Houghton
Mifflin
Harcourt

Math

Grade 7

ISBN 978-0-544-26825-8

11   0928   22 21 20 19 18

4500736916   B C D E F G

Core Skills Math

GRADE 7

Table of Contents

© Houghton Mifflin Harcourt Publishing Company

Table of Contents
Core Skills Math, Grade 7

Mathematics Correlation Chart

Skills	Page Numbers
Algebraic Expressions	26, 27
Angles	37, 38, 39, 40
Area	119, 120, 121, 122
Circles	110, 111, 112, 113, 115, 116, 117, 118
Constructions	42, 43, 44
Data Analysis	6, 7, 8, 9, 10, 11
Operations with Decimals	1, 2, 3, 4
Operations with Fractions	12, 13, 14, 15, 16, 17, 18, 19, 20, 21, 22, 23, 24, 25
Operations with Integers	67, 68, 69, 70, 71, 72, 73, 74, 75, 76, 77, 78, 79
Percent	59, 60, 61, 62, 63, 64, 65, 66
Probability	87, 88, 89, 90, 92, 93, 94, 95, 96, 97, 98, 99, 100, 101, 102, 103, 104, 105
Problem Solving	5, 31, 54, 91, 114, 131, 133, 134, 135, 136
Rational Numbers	80, 81, 82, 83, 84, 85, 86, 130, 132
Ratios, Rates, and Proportions	45, 46, 47, 48, 49, 50, 51
Scale Drawings	52, 53, 55
Similar Figures	56, 57, 58
Simulations	106, 107, 108, 109
Solid Figures	123, 124, 125
Solving One-Variable Equations	28, 29, 30
Solving One-Variable Inequalities	32, 33, 34, 35, 36
Surface Area	126, 127
Triangles	41
Volume	128, 129

Exploring Division: Decimal by Decimal

Place the decimal point in the dividend so that the division problem is changed to a problem with a whole-number divisor. Write zeros if necessary.

1. $0.05\overline{)2.2765}$ $5\overline{)2\,2\,7\,6\,5}$

2. $0.64\overline{)3.2}$ $64\overline{)3\,2}$

3. $81.5\overline{)73.35}$ $815\overline{)7\,3\,3\,5}$

4. $0.072\overline{)417.6}$ $72\overline{)4\,1\,7\,6}$

Estimate. Then find each quotient.

5. $6.8\overline{)12.92}$

6. $2.6\overline{)33.8}$

7. $9.25\overline{)277.5}$

8. $2.24\overline{)2.688}$

9. $4.7\overline{)14.57}$

10. $9.1\overline{)65.52}$

11. $7.12\overline{)291.92}$

12. $3.03\overline{)36.966}$

13. $8.4\overline{)27.72}$

14. $2.3\overline{)158.7}$

15. $5.12\overline{)215.04}$

16. $3.61\overline{)324.9}$

17. $8.5\overline{)249.05}$

18. $0.7\overline{)107.8}$

19. $5.2\overline{)448.812}$

20. $6.4\overline{)210.56}$

Use the given division number sentence to help you predict the missing number. Use a calculator to check your predictions.

> Given: $345 \div 15 = 23$

21. $3.45 \div 0.15 = $ _____

22. $34.5 \div 1.5 = $ _____

23. $0.345 \div 0.015 = $ _____

24. $34.5 \div 0.15 = $ _____

25. $345 \div 1.5 = $ _____

26. $3.45 \div 15 = $ _____

27. $3.45 \div $ _____ $ = 2.3$

28. _____ $\div 15 = 2.3$

LOGICAL REASONING

29. The value of the expression below is 1. Each digit from 1 through 9 is used only once. What are the two missing numbers?

$1.23 + 0.08 - 0.67 + $ _____ $ - $ _____

Using Division

Estimate. Then find each quotient.

1. $3\overline{)45.6}$ 2. $8\overline{)25.52}$ 3. $0.2\overline{)3}$ 4. $0.5\overline{)303}$

5. $4.8\overline{)24.48}$ 6. $0.03\overline{)1.575}$ 7. $1.5\overline{)7.59}$ 8. $0.012\overline{)0.816}$

Estimate. Then find each quotient, rounded to the

nearest whole number: 9. $8.2\overline{)16.6}$ 10. $7\overline{)55.5}$ 11. $7.6\overline{)49.4}$

nearest tenth: 12. $7\overline{)37.9}$ 13. $0.44\overline{)1.26}$ 14. $9.6\overline{)4.527}$

nearest hundredth: 15. $3.2\overline{)6.9}$ 16. $0.18\overline{)0.59}$ 17. $0.47\overline{)64}$

nearest thousandth: 18. $6\overline{)11.8}$ 19. $5\overline{)2.424}$ 20. $13\overline{)20}$

Use the pattern to find each quotient.

21. $2,800 \div 8 = 350$
    $280 \div 8 = 35$

    $28.0 \div 8 =$ _____

    $2.8 \div 8 =$ _____

22. $7,321 \div 0.5 = 14,642$
    $732.1 \div 0.5 = 1,464.2$

    $73.21 \div 0.5 =$ _____

    $7.321 \div 0.5 =$ _____

MIXED APPLICATIONS

23. The Leaning Tower of Pisa is a famous landmark in Italy. Each year it tilts a little farther. During the last century the tilt at the top has increased by about 1.1 millimeters per year. At this rate, by how much would the tilt increase in 15 years?

_____

24. About 800,000 tourists bought tickets to visit the Leaning Tower of Pisa one year. This brought the city about $2 million from ticket sales. Use these figures to estimate the price of one ticket.

_____

NUMBER SENSE

25. You can make up a number pattern with whole numbers and decimals. What are the missing numbers?

_____, 40, _____, 1.6, 0.32, 0.064, 0.0128

Problem-Solving Strategy

GUESS AND CHECK

1. Jerry was 6 years old when his mother was 30. Now she is twice his age. How old is Jerry?

   _____

2. Moria bought $0.65 worth of stamps. She paid for them with 15 coins. What coins did she use?

   _____

MIXED APPLICATIONS

3. An office building has 10 floors of the same height. The ninth floor is how many times as far from the ground as the third floor?

   _____

4. The difference between twice a number and half the number is 30. What is the number?

   _____

5. Lisa sold costume jewelry at a bazaar. The first hour she sold 2 bracelets and 3 rings for a total of $26. Later a customer bought 2 rings and paid $12. All bracelets were priced the same. All rings were priced the same. How much did a bracelet cost?

   _____

6. Tara wants to weigh her three stuffed animals. They will fit on the scale only two at a time. Together, Addie and Blissy weigh 18 ounces, Blissy and Corky weigh 22 ounces, and Addie and Corky weigh 12 ounces. How much does each animal weigh?

   _____

NUMBER SENSE

7. Use any of the digits 1, 3, and 9 and the operation signs + and/or − to write expressions equal to all the whole numbers from 1 through 13. Each digit can be used only once in each expression.

Examples:	Number	Expression
	1	1
	2	3 − 1

   _____ _____ _____ _____

   _____ _____ _____ _____

   _____ _____ _____ _____

Exploring Sample Groups

1. Tell which sample group would better predict the most frequent choice of adults. Explain your answer.

Hiking Club Sample Group Favorite Pastime	
Pastime	Number of Adults
Physical Activity	26
Television Viewing	6
Hobby	8
Other	10

Random Sample Favorite Pastime	
Pastime	Number of Adults
Physical Activity	14
Television Viewing	8
Hobby	12
Other	16

_____

_____

Choose a word or words from the box to complete each sentence.

predict
random
survey
data

2. The _____ collected from a sample group can help

you _____ the most frequent choice of a large group.

3. To find the most frequent choice of a group, conduct a

_____.

4. People with different interests have the same chance of being

chosen when the group is chosen at _____.

MIXED REVIEW

Write <, >, or = for ◯.

5. 4,122 ◯ 4,221

6. 50,002 ◯ 50,200

7. 7.46 ◯ 7.29

8. 37,186 ◯ 37,145

9. 0.03 ◯ 0.30

10. 2.17 ◯ 2.170

Data Collection

Oaksford Middle School surveyed a sample of 100 students. The students were asked which assembly program they liked best during the year. The results of the survey are tallied in the chart. When you make predictions, assume that the sample in the survey was unbiased.

Oaksford Middle School Survey Results		
Favorite Program	**Students**	
	Tally	**Number**
Sing-Along	𝍷𝍷𝍷 𝍷𝍷𝍷 𝍷𝍷𝍷 𝍷𝍷𝍷 𝍷𝍷𝍷 𝍷𝍷𝍷	30
Puppet Show	𝍷𝍷𝍷 𝍷𝍷𝍷 𝍷𝍷𝍷 I	
Story Theater Group	𝍷𝍷𝍷 𝍷𝍷𝍷 𝍷𝍷𝍷 𝍷𝍷𝍷 I	
Magic Show	𝍷𝍷𝍷 𝍷𝍷𝍷 𝍷𝍷𝍷 𝍷𝍷𝍷 𝍷𝍷𝍷 𝍷𝍷𝍷 III	

1. Complete the number column in the table.

2. Suppose Oaksford Middle School has 612 students. Predict how many of them liked the Story Theater Group best.

   _____ _____

3. Of the 612 students, predict how many of them liked the Magic Show best.

   _____

4. Predict how many more of the 612 students liked the Magic Show better than the Sing-Along.

   _____

MIXED APPLICATIONS

5. A school has 789 students. In a random sample of 50 students, 6 make the same choice as you. Predict how many in the school would make this choice.

   _____

6. Tickets to a school play cost $1.50 for a student and $2.50 for an adult. Clara sold 5 tickets for a total of $10.50. How many of these were student tickets?

   _____

VISUAL THINKING

7. Start with the top letter and move down to the left or right, one letter at a time. How many ways can you spell *SHOW*? (One path is shown for you.)

   _____

8. How many ways can you spell *DANCE*?

   _____

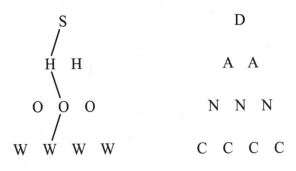

Populations and Samples

1. Paul and his friends average their test grades and find that the average is 95. The teacher announces that the average grade of all of her classes is 83. Why are the averages so different?

   _____

   _____

   _____

2. Nancy hears a report that the average price of gasoline is $2.82. She averages the prices of stations near her home. She finds the average price of gas to be $3.03. Why are the averages different?

   _____

   _____

   _____

Determine whether each sample is a random sample or a biased sample. Explain your reasoning.

3. Carol wants to find out the favorite foods of students at her middle school. She asks the boys' basketball team about their favorite foods.

   _____

   _____

   _____

4. Dallas wants to know what elective subjects the students at his school like best. He surveys students who are leaving band class.

   _____

   _____

   _____

5. A manager samples the receipts of every fifth person who goes through the line. Out of 50 people, 4 had a mispriced item. If 600 people go to this store each day, how many people would you expect to have a mispriced item?

   _____

   _____

   _____

6. Jerry randomly selects 20 boxes of crayons from the shelf and finds 2 boxes with at least one broken crayon. If the shelf holds 130 boxes, how many would you expect to have at least one broken crayon?

   _____

   _____

   _____

Central Tendency

Use the tables for Exercises 1–4.

Students at Everett Middle School are selling boxes of popcorn to raise funds for the science center. The tables show the enrollment and the sales figures for the seventh- and eighth-grade homerooms.

Seventh-Grade Homerooms		
Teacher	Number in Homeroom	Boxes of Popcorn Sold
Mrs. Todd	30	12
Mr. Davis	32	25
Ms. Green	35	32
Mr. Gray	31	24
Ms. Sanchez	32	12

Eighth-Grade Homerooms		
Teacher	Number in Homeroom	Boxes of Popcorn Sold
Mr. Han	33	8
Ms. Gibson	36	28
Mrs. Majia	35	40
Mr. Ray	36	36

1. Which grade has more students, the seventh grade or the eighth grade? How many more students?

_____

2. In which grade is the mean number of students per homeroom greater, the seventh or the eighth grade? How much greater?

_____

3. Find the mean, mode, and median of the number of boxes of popcorn sold in the seventh-grade homerooms.

_____

4. Find the mean, mode, and median of the number of boxes of popcorn sold in the eighth-grade homerooms

_____

MIXED APPLICATIONS

5. In three days Gina sold 15 boxes. On the second day, she sold 1 more than on the first. On the third day, she sold 5 more than on the first. How many boxes did she sell the third day?

_____

6. Mario made five phone calls lasting 4, 6, 8, 15, and 21 minutes. After another call, the median length of the phone calls was 10 minutes. What was the mean length of the six calls?

_____

LOGICAL REASONING

7. Only one girl is telling the truth.

Who are the twins? _____

Eve: "Doris and I are twins."
Ann: "Doris and Eve are not twins."
Doris: "Ann and I are not twins."

Analyzing Data

MEAN, MEDIAN, AND MODE

Find the mean, median, and mode for each set of data. Round the answers for Exercises 1–4 to the nearest hundredth.

1. 70, 72, 75, 75, 78, 80, 80

2. 2.63, 9.61, 3.057, 8.39, 5.12

3. 3lb, 7lb, 5lb

4. 20, 25, 25, 35, 40

Use the data in Exercise 1. Write the number or numbers that you can remove from the set of data to make each statement correct.

5. There is no mode

6. The mode is 80

Write *true* or *false* for each.

7. Some sets of data do not have a mean.

8. There is always a mode for each set of data.

MIXED APPLICATIONS

Tim worked in a store during the summer. The hours he worked one week were 2, 3, 3, 4, 3, 5, and 1.

9. What was the total number of hours he worked during the week?

10. Find the mean, median, and mode for the data.

WRITER'S CORNER

11. Write a problem using the data for Exercises 9–10. Solve.

Comparing Populations

Use the following information to solve Exercises 1–6.

Carol wants to know how many people live in each household in her town. She conducts two random surveys of 10 people each and asks how many people live in their home. Her results are listed below.

Sample A: 1, 6, 2, 4, 4, 3, 5, 5, 2, 8   **Sample B: 3, 4, 5, 4, 3, 2, 4, 5, 4, 4**

1. Make a dot plot for Sample A.

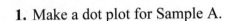
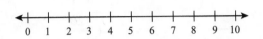

2. Make a dot plot for Sample B.

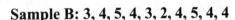
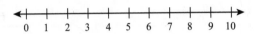

3. Find the mean and MAD for Sample A.

Mean: _____

MAD: _____

4. Find the mean and MAD for Sample B.

Mean: _____

MAD: _____

5. What can you infer about the population based on Sample A? Explain.

_____

_____

6. What can you infer about the population based on Sample B? Explain.

_____

_____

MIXED APPLICATIONS

7. Ana collects data on how many candy bars ten students in her class sold for the fundraiser. The amounts are show in the table.

Candy Bars Sold
15, 10, 10, 5, 12, 20, 15, 5, 10, 10

What are the mean and MAD for these data?

_____

_____

8. Mrs. Saenz wants to know if the words are longer in the old history book or in the new history book. She has her students find the average length of the words by taking a random sample from each book.

Old History Book
4, 8, 6, 3, 5, 4, 2, 7, 5, 9, 3, 4

New History Book
6, 5, 4, 7, 5, 6, 6, 3, 4, 5, 3, 6

What is the next thing Mrs. Saenz must do to get her results?

_____

Adding and Subtracting Fractions

Estimate. Then find each exact sum or difference. Write each answer in simplest form.

1. $\dfrac{1}{3}$
   $+\dfrac{1}{9}$

2. $\dfrac{1}{4}$
   $+\dfrac{7}{8}$

3. $\dfrac{5}{8}$
   $-\dfrac{1}{2}$

4. $\dfrac{2}{3}$
   $-\dfrac{1}{6}$

5. $\dfrac{1}{3}$
   $+\dfrac{7}{12}$

6. $\dfrac{1}{2}$
   $+\dfrac{4}{5}$

7. $\dfrac{5}{6}$
   $-\dfrac{3}{4}$

8. $\dfrac{3}{4}$
   $+\dfrac{5}{6}$

9. $\dfrac{5}{6}$
   $-\dfrac{3}{8}$

10. $\dfrac{4}{5}$
    $+\dfrac{11}{20}$

11. $\dfrac{2}{3} + \dfrac{1}{6} + \dfrac{1}{4}$ _____

12. $\dfrac{1}{2} + \dfrac{5}{6} + \dfrac{3}{8}$ _____

13. $\dfrac{19}{25} - \dfrac{3}{5}$ _____

MIXED APPLICATIONS

14. Althea spent $\dfrac{3}{4}$ of her earnings last month. She spent $\dfrac{1}{4}$ on recreation, $\dfrac{1}{6}$ on art supplies, and the rest on clothes. What part of her earnings did she spend on clothes?

_____

15. The library has enough DVDs to display an equal number of them in groups of 3, 5, or 9. What is the least number of DVDs the library has?

_____

LOGICAL REASONING

Fill in missing numerators. Numerators cannot be zero.

16. The fractions have a sum of 1.
    The numerators have a sum of 4.

17. The fractions have a sum of 1.
    The numerators have a sum of 5.

18. The fractions have a sum of 1.
    The numerators have a sum of 9.

19. The fractions have a sum of 1.
    The numerators have a sum of 5.

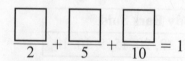

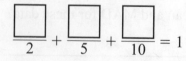

12

Unit 3
Core Skills Math, Grade 7

Adding Mixed Numbers

Find each sum. Write the answer in simplest form.

1. $9\frac{1}{2}$
   $+ 1\frac{1}{2}$

2. 5
   $+ 3\frac{1}{3}$

3. $2\frac{4}{5}$
   $+ 16\frac{2}{5}$

4. $7\frac{1}{2}$
   $+ 2\frac{1}{4}$

5. $8\frac{5}{6}$
   $+ 3\frac{2}{3}$

6. $9\frac{3}{4}$
   $+ 15\frac{1}{2}$

7. $5\frac{1}{12}$
   $+ 2\frac{3}{4}$

8. $21\frac{1}{6}$
   $+ 4\frac{1}{8}$

9. $2\frac{1}{2}$
   $+ 7\frac{5}{6}$

10. $3\frac{7}{10}$
    $+ 9\frac{1}{6}$

11. $16\frac{3}{4}$
    $+ 5\frac{2}{3}$

12. $15\frac{1}{8}$
    $+ 6\frac{1}{10}$

13. $6\frac{3}{4}$
    $+ \frac{5}{6}$

14. $8\frac{4}{5}$
    $+ 1\frac{3}{8}$

15. $10\frac{1}{7}$
    $+ 4\frac{3}{5}$

16. $2\frac{7}{8} + 3\frac{1}{2} + 3\frac{1}{4}$ _____

17. $5\frac{1}{2} + 2\frac{1}{3} + 9\frac{1}{6} + 2$ _____

18. $5\frac{1}{4} + 3\frac{1}{12} + 6 + 4\frac{1}{6}$ _____

19. $2\frac{1}{15} + 7\frac{2}{5} + 4 + 3\frac{1}{3}$ _____

MIXED APPLICATIONS

20. Four friends spent an hour picking strawberries. Jennifer picked $1\frac{5}{6}$ quarts, Ilia picked $1\frac{3}{4}$ quarts, Lee picked $1\frac{1}{2}$ quarts, and Wendy picked $2\frac{1}{8}$ quarts. How many quarts did they pick all together?

_____

21. Five sections of fencing around a garden are 7 yards long, $8\frac{3}{4}$ yards long, $12\frac{1}{2}$ yards long, $15\frac{1}{3}$ yards long, and $7\frac{3}{4}$ yards long. What is the total length of the fencing?

_____

NUMBER SENSE

Use the numbers in the box for Exercises 22–23.

| $\frac{1}{8}$ | $\frac{1}{6}$ | $\frac{1}{4}$ | $\frac{1}{3}$ | $\frac{1}{2}$ | $1\frac{1}{8}$ |

22. Find three different numbers whose sum is 1. _____

23. Find three different numbers whose sum is $\frac{3}{4}$. _____

13

Name _____ Date _____

Adding Fractions and Mixed Numbers

Find each sum. Write the answer in simplest form.

1. $\dfrac{1}{5}$
    $+\dfrac{2}{5}$

2. $\dfrac{9}{15}$
    $+\dfrac{1}{15}$

3. $\dfrac{3}{8}$
    $+\dfrac{1}{2}$

4. $\dfrac{1}{6}$
    $+\dfrac{2}{3}$

5. $\dfrac{4}{9}$
    $+\dfrac{1}{4}$

6. 12
    $+7\dfrac{5}{8}$

7. $3\dfrac{1}{5}$
    $+4\dfrac{3}{4}$

8. $3\dfrac{7}{9}$
    $+2\dfrac{1}{3}$

9. $8\dfrac{2}{5}$
    $+3\dfrac{1}{4}$

10. $2\dfrac{1}{5}$
    $+8\dfrac{2}{3}$

11. $2\dfrac{3}{4}$
    $+1\dfrac{1}{5}$

12. 15
    $+2\dfrac{5}{8}$

13. $\dfrac{4}{5}$
    $+\dfrac{1}{3}$

14. $\dfrac{2}{9}$
    $+\dfrac{1}{6}$

15. $8\dfrac{1}{2}$
    $+5\dfrac{3}{7}$

MIXED APPLICATIONS

16. One day Mr. Oritz drove for $6\dfrac{1}{3}$ hours. The next day, he drove for $9\dfrac{1}{2}$ hours. For how many hours did he drive during the two days?

_____

17. A new swimming pool is being filled. On Monday $404\dfrac{3}{4}$ gallons of water were pumped into the pool. On Tuesday $358\dfrac{3}{5}$ gallons of water were added. How many gallons of water were pumped into the pool?

_____

MATH CONNECTION

A unit fraction is a fraction with 1 as the numerator. Some fractions can be written as the sum of two unit fractions.

Example $\dfrac{5}{8} = \dfrac{1}{8} + \dfrac{4}{8} = \dfrac{1}{8} + \dfrac{1}{2}$ ⟵ _____ $\dfrac{1}{8}$ and $\dfrac{1}{2}$ are unit fractions.

18. Write five more fractions as the sum of two unit fractions.

_____

_____

Subtracting Mixed Numbers

Find each difference. Write each answer in simplest form.

1. $18\frac{1}{3}$
   $-\ 12$
   _____

2. $17\frac{3}{5}$
   $-\ 6\frac{1}{5}$
   _____

3. $9\frac{5}{8}$
   $-\ 7\frac{1}{8}$
   _____

4. $11\frac{5}{9}$
   $-\ 3\frac{2}{9}$
   _____

5. $17\frac{3}{4}$
   $-\ 10\frac{1}{8}$
   _____

6. $12\frac{5}{6}$
   $-\ 5\frac{2}{3}$
   _____

7. $24\frac{3}{5}$
   $-\ 11\frac{3}{10}$
   _____

8. $16\frac{3}{4}$
   $-\ 8\frac{5}{16}$
   _____

9. $10\frac{11}{12}$
   $-\ 6\frac{1}{4}$
   _____

10. $9\frac{7}{8}$
    $-\ 6\frac{13}{24}$
    _____

11. 7
    $-\ 5\frac{1}{6}$
    _____

12. 16
    $-\ 7\frac{3}{8}$
    _____

13. $22\frac{1}{6}$
    $-\ 15\frac{2}{3}$
    _____

14. $10\frac{1}{8}$
    $-\ 9\frac{3}{4}$
    _____

15. $4\frac{3}{10}$
    $-\ 1\frac{4}{5}$
    _____

16. $15 - 3\frac{5}{6}$ _____

17. $6\frac{3}{8} - 5\frac{5}{8}$ _____

18. $9\frac{3}{10} - 5\frac{3}{5}$ _____

MIXED APPLICATIONS

19. Dana spent 3 hours baby-sitting for a neighbor. She and the children played games for $1\frac{3}{4}$ hours and watched TV for $\frac{1}{2}$ hour. The rest of the time, Dana read stories. How much time did Dana spend reading stories?

_____

20. Quincy went to see two one-act plays. With an intermission of $\frac{1}{6}$ hour, the evening lasted $2\frac{1}{2}$ hours. The first play was $1\frac{1}{4}$ hours long. How long did the second play last?

_____

VISUAL THINKING

21. Draw 12 squares by connecting dots in the figure.

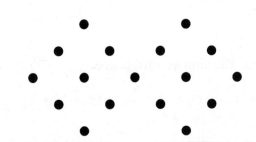

Subtracting Fractions and Mixed Numbers

Find each difference. Write each answer in simplest form.

1. $\dfrac{3}{7}$
    $-\dfrac{1}{7}$

2. $\dfrac{8}{9}$
    $-\dfrac{3}{4}$

3. $\dfrac{11}{12}$
    $-\dfrac{2}{5}$

4. $9\dfrac{1}{6}$
    $-2\dfrac{7}{9}$

5. 9
    $-4\dfrac{3}{8}$

Complete.

6. $6\dfrac{5}{8} - 2\dfrac{\boxed{}}{8} = 4\dfrac{2}{8}$

7. $\dfrac{4}{7} + \dfrac{\boxed{}}{7} = 1$

8. $\dfrac{9}{10} - \dfrac{\boxed{}}{\boxed{}} = \dfrac{1}{5}$

Solve. Write each answer in simplest form.

9. $\dfrac{9}{8} - \dfrac{1}{4} - \dfrac{1}{2}$

10. $10\dfrac{1}{4} - 2\dfrac{1}{8} - \dfrac{1}{12}$

11. $\dfrac{3}{4} + \dfrac{1}{2} - \dfrac{5}{6}$

12. $\dfrac{3}{5} - \dfrac{1}{10} + \dfrac{1}{2}$

_____   _____   _____   _____

MIXED APPLICATIONS

13. In 1963 the spaceflight of Valentina Tereshkova, the first woman in space, lasted $70\dfrac{5}{6}$ hr. In 1961 the spaceflight of Yuri Gagarin, the first man in space, lasted $1\dfrac{4}{5}$ hr. How much longer was Tereshkova's flight than Gagarin's?

_____

14. In a recent year, among people 18 to 24 years old in the United States, $\dfrac{2}{5}$ had four years of high school and $\dfrac{7}{20}$ had at least some college in addition to high school. What fraction of that age group had fewer than four years of high school?

_____

MIXED REVIEW

Compare. Write <, >, or =.

15. $\dfrac{5}{4} \bigcirc \dfrac{3}{2}$

16. $\dfrac{1}{8} \bigcirc \dfrac{1}{10}$

17. $32.6 \bigcirc 3.26$

18. $\dfrac{3}{6} \bigcirc 0.50$

Estimate the sum or difference.

19. $8,901 + 2,009$

20. $9.15 - 3.08$

21. $6\dfrac{5}{6} + 4\dfrac{2}{3}$

22. $\dfrac{11}{12} - \dfrac{2}{5}$

_____   _____   _____   _____

16

Multiplying Fractions

Find each product. Write each answer in simplest form.

1. $\frac{1}{3} \times \frac{3}{8}$ _____

2. $\frac{2}{3} \times \frac{3}{5}$ _____

3. $\frac{5}{12} \times \frac{6}{7}$ _____

4. $\frac{2}{7} \times \frac{7}{8}$ _____

5. $\frac{5}{8} \times \frac{7}{10}$ _____

6. $\frac{4}{5} \times \frac{2}{7}$ _____

7. $\frac{1}{3} \times \frac{3}{5} \times \frac{5}{7}$ _____

8. $\frac{5}{2} \times \frac{2}{3} \times \frac{3}{10}$ _____

9. $\frac{3}{4} \times \frac{4}{5} \times \frac{1}{3}$ _____

10. $\frac{2}{3} \times \frac{7}{10} \times \frac{5}{21}$ _____

11. $\frac{9}{7} \times \frac{5}{9} \times \frac{21}{20}$ _____

12. $\frac{17}{6} \times \frac{5}{34} \times \frac{7}{10}$ _____

Complete. Write <, >, or =.

13. $\frac{6}{5} \times \frac{3}{5} \bigcirc \frac{3}{5}$

14. $\frac{3}{4} \times \frac{7}{8} \bigcirc \frac{7}{8}$

15. $\frac{4}{3} \times \frac{3}{8} \bigcirc \frac{1}{2}$

16. $\frac{3}{5} \times \frac{1}{6} \bigcirc \frac{1}{10}$

17. $\frac{1}{3} \times \frac{4}{5} \bigcirc \frac{4}{5}$

18. $\frac{3}{4} \times \frac{8}{9} \bigcirc \frac{2}{3}$

MIXED APPLICATIONS

19. A gardener uses $\frac{2}{3}$ of a greenhouse for growing roses, with $\frac{3}{8}$ of this space for tea roses. What part of the space is used to grow tea roses?

_____

20. Tiffany spent $\frac{3}{5}$ of her money to buy begonias and $\frac{1}{2}$ of the remaining money to buy peas. What part of her money did she spend on peas?

_____

21. Marvella's uncle paid $26 for 20 plants. Some were carnations, selling at 4 for $3. The rest were zinnias, priced at 3 for $5. How many plants of each type did he buy?

_____

NUMBER SENSE

Find the two numbers in each pair.

22. The sum of two numbers is 10. Their product is 1 less than 5^2.

_____

23. Two numbers differ by 4. Their product is 4 less than 7^2.

_____

More Multiplying Fractions

Choose the pairs of fractions that have a product of 1.

1. $\frac{1}{4} \quad \frac{2}{5} \quad \frac{5}{7} \quad \frac{5}{2} \quad \frac{7}{1} \quad \frac{5}{1} \quad \frac{4}{1}$ _____

2. $\frac{3}{8} \quad \frac{4}{5} \quad \frac{2}{3} \quad \frac{1}{9} \quad \frac{3}{2} \quad \frac{8}{1} \quad \frac{9}{1}$ _____

Find each product. Write each product in simplest form.

3. $\frac{5}{9} \times \frac{9}{5}$ _____

4. $\frac{7}{8} \times \frac{8}{9}$ _____

5. $\frac{5}{16} \times \frac{7}{15}$ _____

6. $\frac{8}{9} \times \frac{9}{8}$ _____

7. $5 \times \frac{9}{5}$ _____

8. $\frac{5}{8} \times \frac{5}{2}$ _____

9. $\frac{1}{4} \times 3$ _____

10. $\frac{7}{8} \times \frac{4}{5}$ _____

11. $\frac{1}{2} \times \frac{8}{9} \times \frac{3}{7}$ _____

12. $\frac{2}{3} \times 6 \times \frac{1}{4}$ _____

13. $\frac{11}{12} \times \frac{6}{25} \times \frac{5}{9}$ _____

Solve.

14. $\frac{1}{2} \times \left(\frac{1}{2} + \frac{1}{4} \right)$ _____

15. $\frac{3}{4} + \frac{1}{8} - \frac{2}{3}$ _____

16. $\frac{7}{10} + \frac{2}{5} \times \frac{1}{4}$ _____

MIXED APPLICATIONS

17. Mona has 20 palm trees. Of these, $\frac{2}{5}$ are royal palms. How many of Mona's palm trees are royal palms?

_____

18. Barney planted $\frac{3}{8}$ of his garden with tulips. Of these, $\frac{2}{9}$ were red tulips. What part of Barney's garden was not planted with red tulips?

_____

MATH CONNECTION

Exponents can be used to indicate repeated multiplication of a fractional factor. Find each product.

19. $\left(\frac{1}{5} \right)^2$ _____

20. $\left(\frac{2}{3} \right)^2$ _____

21. $\left(\frac{2}{5} \right)^3$ _____

22. $\left(\frac{1}{3} \right)^3$ _____

Multiplying Mixed Numbers

Find each product. Write each product in simplest form.

1. $\frac{3}{4} \times 24$ _____

2. $7 \times 2\frac{1}{7}$ _____

3. $17 \times \frac{1}{3}$ _____

4. $9 \times 4\frac{1}{3}$ _____

5. $\frac{1}{2} \times 2\frac{1}{4}$ _____

6. $7\frac{1}{2} \times 1\frac{1}{3}$ _____

7. $6\frac{2}{3} \times 2\frac{1}{4}$ _____

8. $2\frac{2}{3} \times 3\frac{1}{8}$ _____

9. $\frac{3}{7} \times 5\frac{1}{4}$ _____

10. $2 \times 6\frac{2}{5}$ _____

11. $4\frac{1}{3} \times 1\frac{1}{2}$ _____

12. $2\frac{4}{7} \times \frac{5}{9}$ _____

13. $3\frac{1}{5} \times 2\frac{1}{4}$ _____

14. $9\frac{3}{4} \times 2\frac{2}{13}$ _____

15. $37\frac{1}{2} \times 1\frac{3}{5}$ _____

16. $\frac{5}{8} \times 1\frac{4}{5} \times 1\frac{7}{9}$ _____

17. $1\frac{1}{3} \times 1\frac{2}{5} \times 1\frac{1}{2}$ _____

18. $\frac{1}{3} \times \frac{1}{7} \times 4\frac{2}{3}$ _____

19. $5 \times 2\frac{1}{10} \times 2\frac{1}{7}$ _____

MIXED APPLICATIONS

20. At the circus $\frac{1}{8}$ of the performers were trapeze artists. Of these, $\frac{2}{3}$ were women. What part of the circus performers were women trapeze artists?

_____

21. Jim and his uncle went to the circus. Together they spent $30: $\frac{4}{15}$ for a bus ride, $\frac{2}{5}$ for food, $7 for tickets, and the rest on souvenirs. What part of their money did they spend on souvenirs?

_____

NUMBER SENSE

Fill in two numbers that make each inequality true.

22. Use multiples of 3 that differ by 3. $(\frac{2}{3} \times$ _____$) < 11 < (\frac{2}{3} \times$ _____$)$

23. Use multiples of 4 that differ by 4. $(\frac{3}{4} \times$ _____$) < 17 < (\frac{3}{4} \times$ _____$)$

24. Use multiples of 5 that differ by 5. $(\frac{4}{5} \times$ _____$) < 30 < (\frac{4}{5} \times$ _____$)$

More Multiplying Mixed Numbers

Find each product. Write each product in simplest form.

1. $10 \times 4\frac{1}{2}$ _____

2. $\frac{4}{9} \times 2\frac{1}{5}$ _____

3. $\frac{9}{11} \times 4$ _____

4. $2\frac{2}{3} \times 7$ _____

5. $7 \times 3\frac{5}{7}$ _____

6. $\frac{2}{3} \times 9\frac{1}{2}$ _____

7. $5\frac{1}{3} \times 6\frac{1}{2}$ _____

8. $4\frac{3}{5} \times 7\frac{3}{4}$ _____

9. $3\frac{2}{3} \times 9\frac{3}{8}$ _____

10. $\frac{1}{2} \times 2\frac{1}{4} \times 1\frac{1}{6}$ _____

11. $1\frac{1}{8} \times 2\frac{1}{4} \times \frac{12}{20}$ _____

Use a calculator to find each product for Exercises 12–14.

12. $\frac{5}{8} \times \frac{2}{5}$ _____

13. $\frac{1}{2} \times \frac{3}{4}$ _____

14. $1\frac{4}{5} \times 2\frac{3}{8}$ _____

15. The product of $2\frac{1}{4} \times 3\frac{1}{2}$ is $7\frac{7}{8}$. Find two other numbers that have a product of $7\frac{7}{8}$.

_____

MIXED APPLICATIONS

16. April spread $12\frac{1}{2}$ pounds of mulch. Ron spread $2\frac{1}{5}$ times as much. How much mulch did Ron spread?

_____

17. Yoko worked $1\frac{1}{4}$ as long on the hydroponic garden project as Mark did. Mark worked on the project for $4\frac{3}{8}$ hours. For how many hours did Yoko and Mark work on the project?

_____

MIXED REVIEW

Estimate each product.

18. 196×9 _____

19. 8.2×12.9 _____

20. $\frac{7}{8} \times \frac{5}{6}$ _____

21. $4\frac{1}{4} \times 9\frac{4}{5}$ _____

22. 2.5×0.48 _____

23. 15.8×1.9 _____

24. $1\frac{7}{9} \times \frac{8}{9}$ _____

25. $\frac{3}{4} \times 77$ _____

Exploring Division with Fractions

Use the fraction-bar model for each division. Write each quotient.

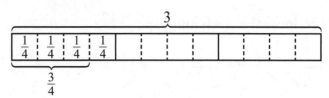

1. $3 \div \frac{3}{4}$ _____

2. $2 \div \frac{1}{4}$ _____

3. $2\frac{1}{4} \div \frac{1}{4}$ _____

Use the number line to model each division problem. Write each quotient.

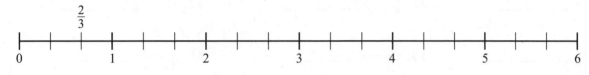

4. $2 \div \frac{2}{3}$ _____

5. $6 \div \frac{2}{3}$ _____

6. $5\frac{1}{3} \div \frac{4}{3}$ _____

Use equivalent fractions and the fraction-bar model to find each quotient.

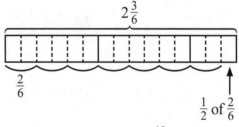

7. Count how many groups of $\frac{2}{6}$ are in $2\frac{3}{6}$.

$2\frac{1}{2} \div \frac{1}{3}$ _____

8. Count how many groups of $\frac{3}{12}$ are in $\frac{10}{12}$.

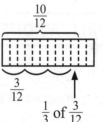

$\frac{5}{6} \div \frac{1}{4}$ _____

Think of a number line to model each division problem. Write each quotient.

9. $4 \div \frac{2}{3}$ _____

10. $2\frac{2}{3} \div \frac{1}{3}$ _____

11. $3\frac{1}{3} \div \frac{2}{3}$ _____

Think of fraction bars to model each division problem. Use equivalent fractions if necessary. Write each quotient.

12. $3 \div \frac{1}{2}$ _____

13. $5 \div \frac{1}{4}$ _____

14. $\frac{1}{2} \div \frac{1}{6}$ _____

VISUAL THINKING

15. Look for a pattern. Draw the missing rectangle.

Unit 3
Core Skills Math, Grade 7

Dividing Fractions

Write the reciprocal of each number.

1. $\frac{1}{7}$ _____   2. 6 _____   3. $1\frac{1}{8}$ _____   4. $3\frac{1}{3}$ _____   5. $2\frac{1}{4}$ _____   6. $\frac{2}{5}$ _____

Find each quotient. Write each answer in simplest form.

7. $6 \div \frac{1}{2}$ _____   8. $7 \div \frac{1}{3}$ _____   9. $\frac{3}{5} \div \frac{1}{4}$ _____

10. $\frac{1}{3} \div \frac{1}{9}$ _____   11. $\frac{3}{8} \div \frac{3}{4}$ _____   12. $12 \div \frac{3}{4}$ _____

13. $\frac{1}{4} \div \frac{1}{5}$ _____   14. $\frac{5}{12} \div \frac{2}{3}$ _____   15. $\frac{7}{8} \div \frac{1}{2}$ _____

16. $\frac{8}{9} \div \frac{1}{3}$ _____   17. $\frac{7}{8} \div \frac{1}{8}$ _____   18. $\frac{3}{10} \div \frac{2}{5}$ _____

19. $\frac{1}{5} \div \frac{7}{10}$ _____   20. $\frac{9}{2} \div \frac{3}{4}$ _____   21. $\frac{3}{5} \div \frac{6}{1}$ _____

Complete.

22. $0.2 \times$ _____ $= 1$ 23. $0.1 \times$ _____ $= 1$ 24. $0.125 \times$ _____ $= 1$

MIXED APPLICATIONS

25. A library in Washington, D.C., has a Dial-a-Story program. When you call, you can hear a $3\frac{1}{2}$-minute folktale. How many times can the complete story be repeated in 1 hour?

_____

26. A library shelf is 9 feet wide. A set of nature books fills $\frac{1}{6}$ of the shelf space. Each book in the set is $\frac{3}{5}$-inch thick. How many books are in the set?

_____

MIXED REVIEW

Solve. Write each answer in simplest form.

27. $\frac{3}{5} + \frac{5}{8}$ _____   28. $2\frac{1}{5} - \frac{3}{4}$ _____   29. $2\frac{1}{2} \times 4\frac{1}{4}$ _____

30. $3\frac{2}{3} \div \frac{3}{4}$ _____   31. $\frac{7}{8} + \frac{5}{12} - \frac{3}{4}$ _____   32. $\left(\frac{4}{7} \times \frac{3}{5}\right) \div 3$ _____

22

More Dividing Fractions

Find each quotient. Write each quotient in simplest form.

1. $\frac{2}{3} \div \frac{8}{15}$ _____

2. $8 \div \frac{4}{5}$ _____

3. $\frac{7}{12} \div \frac{9}{17}$ _____

4. $\frac{9}{10} \div 9$ _____

5. $\frac{23}{24} \div \frac{9}{15}$ _____

6. $\frac{7}{8} \div \frac{7}{15}$ _____

7. $\frac{1}{9} \div \frac{9}{10}$ _____

8. $\frac{2}{5} \div 18$ _____

9. $12 \div \frac{3}{4}$ _____

10. $\frac{1}{2} \div 24$ _____

11. $\frac{5}{7} \div \frac{13}{14}$ _____

12. $\frac{9}{20} \div \frac{5}{6}$ _____

Solve. Write each answer in simplest form.

13. $\frac{5}{6} - \left(\frac{1}{2} \div \frac{3}{4}\right)$ _____

14. $\frac{5}{4} \div \frac{3}{4} - \frac{1}{5}$ _____

MIXED APPLICATIONS

15. How many boards, each $\frac{3}{4}$ yd long, can be cut from a piece of wood that is 6 yards long? Will there be any wood left over?

_____

16. John can wash $\frac{1}{4}$ of a car in 1 minute. How many cars can he wash in 19 minutes?

_____

NUMBER SENSE

Use the numbers to write a fraction division problem with a quotient equal to the number in the box.

17. 1, 3, 4, 8 $\boxed{1\frac{1}{2}}$ _____

18. 4, 9, 24 $\boxed{54}$ _____

19. 2, 4, 7, 9 $\boxed{1\frac{5}{9}}$ _____

20. 2, 3, 6, 7 $\boxed{\frac{7}{9}}$ _____

21. 5, 10, 12 $\boxed{24}$ _____

22. 2, 7, 8, 13 $\boxed{2\frac{2}{13}}$ _____

Name _____   Date _____

Dividing Mixed Numbers

Find each quotient. Write each answer in simplest form.

1. $\frac{1}{3} \div 5$ _____

2. $1\frac{3}{5} \div \frac{3}{5}$ _____

3. $2\frac{1}{8} \div \frac{1}{4}$ _____

4. $\frac{2}{3} \div 2\frac{1}{3}$ _____

5. $\frac{5}{6} \div 1\frac{1}{4}$ _____

6. $8 \div 5\frac{1}{3}$ _____

7. $3\frac{4}{7} \div \frac{5}{7}$ _____

8. $21 \div 2\frac{1}{3}$ _____

9. $5\frac{1}{4} \div \frac{1}{2}$ _____

10. $\frac{7}{8} \div 1\frac{1}{6}$ _____

11. $1\frac{3}{5} \div 8$ _____

12. $15 \div 2\frac{1}{12}$ _____

13. $9\frac{3}{4} \div 1\frac{5}{8}$ _____

14. $7\frac{5}{6} \div \frac{5}{6}$ _____

15. $5\frac{1}{2} \div \frac{1}{6}$ _____

16. $10\frac{2}{5} \div 2\frac{3}{5}$ _____

17. $7\frac{1}{3} \div \frac{5}{6}$ _____

18. $15\frac{3}{4} \div 3\frac{1}{2}$ _____

19. $16\frac{2}{3} \div 6\frac{1}{4}$ _____

20. $12\frac{3}{5} \div \frac{9}{10}$ _____

21. $1\frac{3}{4} \div 4\frac{2}{3}$ _____

22. $9\frac{3}{4} \div 2\frac{1}{6}$ _____

23. $\frac{3}{10} \div 2\frac{2}{5}$ _____

24. $4\frac{4}{5} \div 1\frac{4}{5}$ _____

25. $3\frac{1}{21} \div 2\frac{2}{7}$ _____

26. $11\frac{1}{9} \div \frac{5}{6}$ _____

27. $8\frac{1}{6} \div 2\frac{1}{3}$ _____

MIXED APPLICATIONS

28. Lee has a $1\frac{1}{2}$-pound supply of Kitty Biscuit Treats. Each day he gives his cats $\frac{1}{8}$ pound of the biscuits. For how many days will his supply last?

_____

29. Lee's kitten, Sophia, is $2\frac{1}{3}$ times as heavy as she was last year. Sophia now weighs 21 ounces. What did she weigh a year ago?

_____

LOGICAL REASONING

30. Find the numbers $\triangle$ and $\square$ if $(1\frac{3}{5} \times \triangle) + (\frac{3}{5} \times \square) = 5$

and $(1\frac{3}{5} \times \square) + (\frac{3}{5} \times \triangle) = 6$.

$\triangle =$ _____ $\square =$ _____

More Dividing Mixed Numbers

Find each quotient. Write each quotient in simplest form.

1. $9 \div 3\frac{1}{3}$ _____

2. $7\frac{2}{3} \div 8$ _____

3. $\frac{3}{5} \div 9$ _____

4. $6 \div 2\frac{2}{3}$ _____

5. $6\frac{3}{5} \div 1\frac{3}{5}$ _____

6. $12 \div 2\frac{2}{3}$ _____

7. $2\frac{1}{6} \div 9\frac{3}{4}$ _____

8. $\frac{5}{8} \div 4\frac{3}{5}$ _____

9. $\frac{4}{3} \div 7\frac{1}{3}$ _____

10. $8\frac{1}{2} \div 4\frac{5}{9}$ _____

11. $\frac{2}{3} \div 1\frac{1}{3}$ _____

12. $7\frac{4}{5} \div 6\frac{1}{2}$ _____

13. $5 \div 8\frac{1}{3}$ _____

14. $8\frac{2}{9} \div 1\frac{2}{3}$ _____

15. $15 \div 6\frac{2}{5}$ _____

MIXED APPLICATIONS

16. Pierre bought a $64\frac{1}{2}$-oz bag of dog food. He feeds his dog $10\frac{2}{4}$ oz at each serving. How many full servings are in the bag of dog food?

_____

17. Hulda has a $6\frac{2}{3}$-ft length of rope. She wants to cut it into 4 equal lengths. How long will each length of rope be?

_____

MATH CONNECTION

Compare. Write = or ≠.

18. $\left(\frac{7}{8} \times \frac{4}{5}\right) \times 1\frac{3}{4} \bigcirc \frac{7}{8} \times \left(\frac{4}{5} \times 1\frac{3}{4}\right)$

19. $\left(\frac{7}{8} \div \frac{4}{5}\right) \div 1\frac{3}{4} \bigcirc \frac{7}{8} \div \left(\frac{4}{5} \div 1\frac{3}{4}\right)$

20. $3\frac{2}{3} \times \left(\frac{3}{7} \times \frac{9}{11}\right) \bigcirc \left(3\frac{2}{3} \times \frac{3}{7}\right) \times \frac{9}{11}$

21. $3\frac{2}{3} \div \left(\frac{3}{7} \div \frac{9}{11}\right) \bigcirc \left(3\frac{2}{3} \div \frac{3}{7}\right) \div \frac{9}{11}$

22. How does the Associative Property apply to multiplication and division with fractions and mixed numbers? Explain.

_____

Algebraic Expressions

Add or subtract each expression.

1. $(4.8x + 15.5) + (2.1x - 12.2)$ **2.** $(7x + 8) - (3x + 12)$ **3.** $\left(\frac{1}{2}x + \frac{3}{4}\right) + \left(\frac{1}{2}x - \frac{1}{4}\right)$

_____   _____   _____

Each week, Joey gets paid $10 plus $2 for each chore he does. His sister Julie gets paid $5 plus $3 per chore.

4. Write an expression for how much their parents pay Joey and Julie each week if they do the same amount of chores.

_____

5. If Joey and Julie each do 5 chores, how much do they get paid individually? How much do their parents pay all together?

_____

6. A company sets up a food booth and a game booth at the county fair. The fee for the food booth is $100 plus $5 per day. The fee for the game booth is $50 plus $7 per day. How much does the company pay for both booths for 5 days?

_____

7. A group of people go out to eat. They decide to split the bill so each person pays $\frac{1}{4}$ of the total price. Each of the four people order an appetizer for $6 and a main dish for $9. Write an expression to show how much each person pays.

_____

Multiply each expression.

8. $12(2 + 3x)$ **9.** $5(x - 5)$ **10.** $2(6x + 5)$ **11.** $10(x - 6)$

_____   _____   _____   _____

Complete.

12. $7(6 + y) = (\square \times 6) + (7 \times \square)$ _____

13. $(3 \times z) + (\square \times 4) = 3(\square + \square)$ _____

Rewriting Expressions

Solve.

1. To make a profit, a store manager must mark up the prices on the items being sold. A sports store buys skateboards from a supplier for *s* dollars. The store's manager decides to mark up the price for retail sale by 42%.

   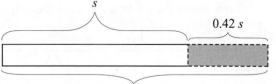

   The markup is _____ % of the price, *s*.

   Find the amount of the markup. Use a bar model.

   The white bar represents the cost of the skateboard from the supplier. _____.

   The gray section is _____% of _____. This can be written as a decimal, _____.

   Add _____ to the cost of the skateboard to find the retail price.

   Retail price = _____ + _____
                    Original cost   Markup

   You can combine like terms in the expression and write the retail price as a single term.

   Retail price = _____

2. What are the benefits of writing the price as the sum of two terms? What are the benefits of writing the price as one term?

   _____

   _____

   _____

3. The markup is changed to 34%; how does the expression for the retail price change?

   _____

MIXED APPLICATIONS

4. Rick buys remote control cars to resell. He applies a markup of 10%. Write two expressions that represent the price of the cars.

   _____

5. Jane sells pillows. For a sale she marks them down 5%. Write two expressions that represent the sale price of the pillows. If a pillow originally costs $15, what is the sale price?

   _____

Exploring Equations

There are 9 cubes in the right pan and 2 cubes visible in the left pan. Let c = the number of cubes not visible in the left pan. The pans are balanced.

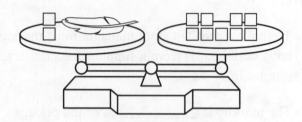

1. Write an algebraic expression to describe how many cubes you have on the left pan.

_____

2. Write an equation to describe the relationship between the number of cubes in the left pan and the number of cubes in the right pan.

_____

3. Suppose you remove 2 cubes from each pan. How many cubes are now on the right pan?

_____

4. How many cubes must now be on the left pan?

_____

5. What is the value of the variable c?

_____

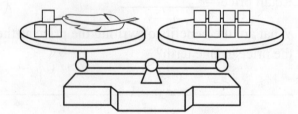

6. Explain how you would find the number of hidden cubes on the pan balance.

_____

Solve each equation.

7. $x + 9 = 21$ _____   **8.** $c + 7 = 14$ _____   **9.** $3 + a = 6$ _____

WRITER'S CORNER

10. Write a word sentence to describe Exercise 6.

_____

_____

28

Using Integers to Solve Equations

Write what you would do to each side of the equation to solve.

1. $x - {-5} = 7$

_____

2. $n + 5 = -2$

_____

3. $3w = -27$

_____

4. $-8t = -120$

_____

5. $z \div 3 = -3$

_____

6. $r + {-6} = -7$

_____

Solve.

7. $n - {-2} = 8$

_____

8. $x + {-7} = -4$

_____

9. $y - 6 = -18$

_____

10. $t + {-9} = 5$

_____

11. $6y = -18$

_____

12. $-4a = {-36}$

_____

13. $-7c = 56$

_____

14. $11y = 33$

_____

15. $9r = -63$

_____

16. $-300x = 900$

_____

17. $15z = -105$

_____

18. $-2,100t = -6,300$

_____

MIXED APPLICATIONS

19. The attendance at the Jazz Festival has decreased by 74 people each year for the last 3 years. How many fewer people attended the festival this year than attended 3 years ago?

_____

20. Three times a number minus 2 is 25. What is the number?

_____

LOGICAL REASONING

21. Carlos rode the elevator up 4 floors, then down 2 floors. He then rode down 5 more floors and got off on the first floor. Where was Carlos when he began his elevator ride?

_____

Solving Equations

Solve each equation.

1. $4x + 12 = 60$

2. $5(3x - 4) = 40$

3. $\frac{x}{3} = 33$

4. $\frac{8x}{2} = 24$

5. $2(-3x - 4) = 100$

6. $\frac{-2x}{5} = 2$

7. For 15 weeks, Sue put the same amount of money in a jar. Then she took $9 out to spend on a friend's birthday present. She had $21 left. How much did she put in each week?

_____

8. Matt gave half of his books to the local library and kept the other half. His best friend gave him 3 more books. He now has 57 books. How many did he have to start?

_____

9. Half of Allen's test score plus 8 equals 50. What did Allen score on his test?

_____

10. Carl is paid $10 plus $8 an hour. He was paid $66. How many hours did he work?

_____

11. Barry swam three times as many laps as George plus one more lap. Barry swam 25 laps. How many laps did George swim?

_____

12. Gayle has 3 less than two times as many stickers as Robin. Gayle has 25 stickers. How many does Robin have?

_____

13. Mika used the formula $A = \frac{(b_1 + b_2)h}{2}$ to find the area of a trapezoid. What is the length of the base, b_1, if the area is 32 cm², the height is 4 cm, and the length of b_2 is 6 cm?

_____

Solving Problems with Equations and Inequalities

Solve.

1. Mary got $\frac{8}{10}$ of the questions right on her test. With what percentage increase could her score have been at least a 90?

_____

2. Joe's balance in his checking account at the beginning of the month was $132. At the end of the month, it was 15.3% higher. What was his balance at the end of the month?

_____

3. Diane is centering a $3\frac{1}{2}$-inch-long picture on a 12-inch-wide scrapbook page. How far from the side edges should she put the picture?

_____

4. The quarterback was sacked x yards from his own goal as the first quarter ended. He walked to the other end of the field and lined up on the other x yard line. He walked $41\frac{3}{4}$ yards between the two yard lines. How far from his end zone was he sacked? Hint: A football field is 100 yards long.

_____

5. Last year, Mr. Jones made $30,000. His boss just informed him that he will be receiving at least an 11.2% raise for this year. How much will he make this year?

_____

6. In March, a share of stock was worth $55. Six months later the value of the stock decreased by 7.2%. Find the final value of the stock.

_____

7. There were 348 students in the school last year. The school expects a 7.25% increase in enrollment this year. How many students are expected to be in the school this year?

_____

8. A company has 350 workers. The president of the company wants to know what percent increase in employment would be necessary for the number of workers to be greater than 375.

_____

Exploring Inequalities

1. Write an inequality to describe the relationship between the number of cubes on the left pan and the number of cubes on the right pan. Let c = the number of hidden cubes on the left pan.

_____

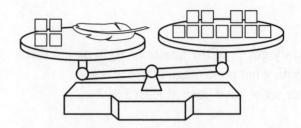

2. Explain how you would find the possible numbers of hidden cubes.

_____

_____

3. Solve the inequality.

_____

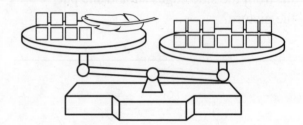

4. Explain how to find the possible number of hidden cubes on the pan balance.

_____

_____

Solve each inequality.

5. $y + 7 < 11$ 6. $n + 2 > 4$ 7. $z + 3 < 8$

_____   _____   _____

MIXED REVIEW

Use equivalent fractions to compare. Write <, >, or =.

8. $\frac{2}{3} \bigcirc \frac{6}{7}$ 9. $\frac{3}{5} \bigcirc \frac{4}{7}$ 10. $\frac{6}{5} \bigcirc \frac{5}{4}$

Find each product.

11.	56	12.	0.5	13.	1.4	14.	0.002	15.	0.73
	$\times\ 0.2$		$\times\ 0.5$		$\times\ 3$		$\times\ 4.1$		$\times\ 4.6$

Solving One-Step Inequalities

Solve. Write the whole numbers that make each inequality true.

1. $3a < 15$

_____

2. $b + 12 \leq 19$

_____

3. $c - 7 \geq 0$

_____

4. $\dfrac{d}{4} > 1$

_____

5. $4k \geq 36$

_____

6. $x + 6 < 9$

_____

7. $4n \neq 12$

_____

8. $15 > 3y$

_____

9. $p - 11 \geq 2$

_____

MIXED APPLICATIONS

Write an inequality for each problem. Then solve.

10. Hal wrote a check for $30. After writing the check, he had less than $450. How much did he have in the account before writing the check?

_____

11. Six workers were paid less than $828 for a job. The money was shared equally among them. Could each one have received $138? Explain.

_____

LOGICAL REASONING

Assume that the given statement is true. Write *true*, *false*, *possible*, or *cannot tell* for each conclusion. Explain.

Statement: The Hoopsters won more than 12 basketball games.

12. Conclusion: The Hoopsters played only 12 basketball games

_____

13. Conclusion: The Hoopsters won more games than they lost.

_____

More One-Step Inequalities

Solve and graph each inequality.

1. $a + 5 < 4$

2. $b - 9 > 5$

3. $4c - 3 < 3$

_____

_____

_____

4. $\frac{4}{5}d \geq 8$

5. $e - 2 < 3$

6. $-2t < 14$

_____

_____

_____

7. $-4t \geq 3$

8. $-5y < 10$

9. $s + 2 < 8$

MIXED APPLICATIONS

Write an inequality for Exercise 10. Then solve.

10. At Mac's Sporting Goods, the number of bicycles sold in May was 40 less than the number sold in April. The total number sold in both months was less than the 120 bicycles sold in March. How many were sold in April and May?

_____

_____

11. Barbara rides her bicycle $2\frac{1}{3}$ mi each morning to deliver newspapers. How many miles does she ride in a week?

_____

MIXED REVIEW

Find the sum or difference.

12. $-\frac{1}{4} - -\frac{5}{8}$ _____

13. $-3 + -\frac{4}{7}$ _____

14. $-\frac{4}{9} + \frac{7}{12}$ _____

15. $8 - -4$ _____

16. $-94 - 15$ _____

17. $19 + -9$ _____

Solving Inequalities

Solve each inequality.

1. $3x \geq -12$ 2. $-4x > 16$ 3. $\frac{x}{-2} > -6$ 4. $3.5x \leq 14$

_____ _____ _____ _____

5. Karen divided her books onto 6 shelves. There were at least 14 books per shelf. How many books does she have? Write an inequality to represent the situation. Then solve.

_____

6. A student's solution to the inequality $\frac{x}{-9} > 5$ was $x > -45$. What error did the student make in the solution?

_____

Use the following information to solve Exercises 7–10.

Lina bought 4 smoothies at a health food store. The bill was less than $16.

7. Write and solve an inequality to represent the cost of each smoothie.

_____

8. Is the graph of the solution set a solid ray or individual points? Explain.

_____

_____

9. Does it make sense for the cost of each smoothie to be $0 or less than $0? Explain.

_____

_____

10. Graph the solution set.

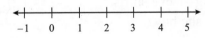

Name _____ Date _____

Solving Two-Step Inequalities

Solve each inequality. Round to the nearest hundredth, if necessary.

1. $10x + 4 \geq -6$

2. $-3x - 21 > 16$

3. $\frac{x}{2} + 1 \geq 4\frac{1}{2}$

_____

_____

_____

4. $\frac{x}{-5} + 11 < 15$

5. $1.5x - 2 \leq 16$

6. $0.2 > -1.2x - 5.1$

_____

_____

_____

Solve each inequality. Then graph the solution set.

7. $-5x - 17 \leq 38$

8. $42 < -\frac{y}{9} + 30$

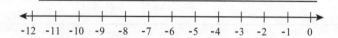

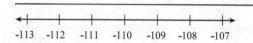

Use the following information to solve Exercises 9 and 10.

Dominique has $5.00. Bagels cost $0.60 each, and a small container of cream cheese costs $1.50.

9. How many bagels can Dominique buy if she also buys one small container of cream cheese? Explain your answer.

_____

_____

10. Graph the solution set.

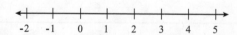

MIXED APPLICATIONS

Use the table for Exercises 11 and 12.

11. Yasmine has $200 to spend on clothes. She decides to purchase a jacket and some long-sleeve shirts. How many long-sleeve shirts can she buy?

_____

Item	Price ($)
Short-sleeve shirt	15
Long-sleeve shirt	20
Pair of jeans	30
Jacket	50

12. Alex has $200 to spend on clothes. She wants to buy a jacket, 2 long-sleeve shirts, and some short-sleeve shirts. Can she buy at least 8 short-sleeve shirts? Explain.

_____

Exploring Angles

Find the measure of each angle.

1. _____

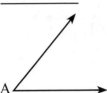
A

2. _____

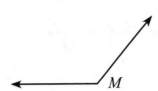
M

3. _____

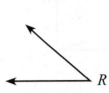
R

4. Which two angles together form complementary angles? _____

5. Which two angles together form supplementary angles? _____

Name the angles. Write *acute*, *right*, or *obtuse*.

6. _____

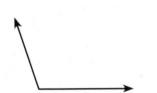

7. _____

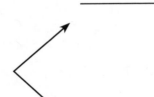

8. _____

9. _____

10. _____

11. _____

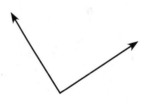

Use a protractor for Exercises 12–13.

12. Draw two complementary angles, one of which measures 30°.

13. Draw two supplementary angles, one of which measures 120°.

_____

_____

LOGICAL REASONING

14. If ∠D and ∠E are complementary angles, and if ∠D and ∠F are supplementary angles, can ∠F be an acute angle? Give a reason for your answer.

_____

Name _____ Date _____

Angles and Angle Pairs

Find the missing measures.

1.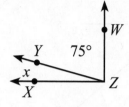

_____

2.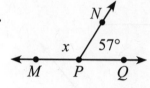

_____

3.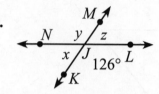

_____

Draw the angle that is the complement and the angle that is the supplement of the angle with the given measure.

4. 30°   5. 85°   6. 25°   7. 78°

MIXED APPLICATIONS

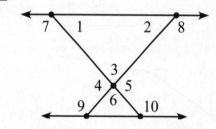

8. The measure of ∠3 is 73°. What are the measures of ∠4, ∠6, and ∠5?

_____

_____

_____

9. Name two pairs of supplementary angles.

_____

_____

_____

LOGICAL REASONING

10. True or false: ∠A is congruent to ∠B. If ∠A is acute, then ∠B is acute.

_____

Angles and Their Measures

Give the measures of the complement and the supplement of each angle.

1. 80°

2. 25°

3. 68°

4. 43°

_____ _____ _____ _____

Use the drawing to answer Exercises 5–9.

5. Name an angle that is adjacent and

complementary to ∠DEF. _____

6. What is the measure of ∠ABD? _____

7. Name an angle that is adjacent and

supplementary to ∠ABD. _____

8. Name an angle that is supplementary to
∠EFD but not adjacent to ∠EFD.

_____

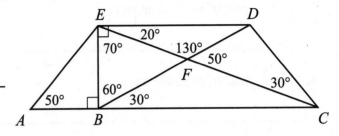

9. Name two pairs of vertical angles.

_____

MIXED APPLICATIONS

10. At 4:00, what are the measures of the two
angles formed by the hands of a clock?

_____

_____

11. ∠A and ∠B are complementary angles.
The measure of ∠B is 70°. What is the
measure of the supplement of ∠A?

_____

VISUAL THINKING

12. The measure of ∠APB is 20°. When $\overrightarrow{PC}$ is drawn, ∠BPC measures 50°.
What is the measure of ∠APC? There are two possible answers. Show
two ways to draw $\overrightarrow{PC}$ and give both answers.

measure of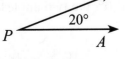

∠APC: _____

measure of

∠APC: _____

Angle Pairs

Use the figure to answer Exercises 1–5.

1. m∠QUP + m∠PUT = _____

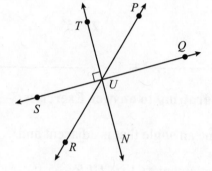

2. Name a pair of supplementary angles.

_____

3. Name a pair of vertical angles.

_____

4. Name a pair of adjacent angles.

_____

5. What is the measure of ∠QUN? Explain your answer.

_____

_____

Solve for the indicated angle measure or variable.

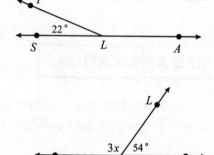

6. m ∠YLA = _____

7. x = _____

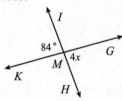

8. Find the value of x and m∠JML.

x = _____ m∠JML = 3x = _____.

MIXED APPLICATIONS

9. The railroad tracks meet the road as shown. The town will allow a parking lot at angle J if the measure of angle J is greater than 38°. Can a parking lot be built at angle J? Why or why not?

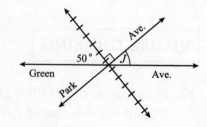

_____

10. A student states that when the sum of two angle measures equals 180°, the two angles are complementary. Explain why the student is incorrect.

_____

40

Triangles

Classify each triangle according to the measures of its angles.

1. 55°, 25°, 100°   **2.** 68°, 90°, 22°   **3.** 20°, 75°, 85°   **4.** 25°, 70°, 85°

_____   _____   _____   _____

5. 50°, 40°, 90°   **6.** 30°, 60°, 90°   **7.** 110°, 30°, 40°   **8.** 45°, 45°, 90°

_____   _____   _____   _____

9. 42°, 78°, 60°   **10.** 40°, 50°, 90°   **11.** 91°, 44°, 45°   **12.** 15°, 82°, 83°

_____   _____   _____   _____

Classify each triangle according to the lengths of its sides.

13. 15 ft, 12 ft, 15 ft   **14.** 7 m, 9 m, 11 m   **15.** 8 cm, 5 cm, 8 cm

_____   _____   _____

16. 14 cm, 9 cm, 7 cm   **17.** 10 m, 6 m, 10 m   **18.** 12 ft, 12 ft, 12 ft

_____   _____   _____

MIXED APPLICATIONS

19. In a triangle, the angle measures have a sum of 180°. If one angle measures 30° and the second angle has twice the measure of the third angle, what are the measures of the second and third angles?

_____

20. Tai is fencing a triangular garden plot. He wants 5 posts along each side. What is the least number of posts that Tai will need?

_____

VISUAL THINKING

21. Draw line segments to show how the figure can be separated into 8 congruent equilateral triangles.

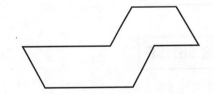

Constructing Segments and Angles

Construct a figure congruent to the given figure.

1.

2.
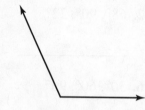

3.

4.

Draw each figure, using a ruler and a protractor. Then use the figure to construct a congruent figure, using a compass and a straightedge.

5. a 6-cm line segment

6. a 120° angle

MIXED APPLICATIONS

7. Construct triangle *ABC* by constructing line segments and an angle congruent to the figures shown.

8. The measure of an angle is 40° more than the measure of its supplement. Find the measure of the angle and its supplement.

_____

_____

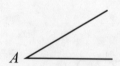

NUMBER SENSE

9. The square of twice a number is equal to the number taken to the third power minus the number squared. What is the number?

_____

Constructing Triangles

Construct a triangle for each set of angle measurements using a protractor and a straightedge.

1. 30°, 60°, 90°   **2.** 45°, 50°, 85°   **3.** 20°, 60°, 100°   **4.** 60°, 60°, 60°

Use the given segments to construct each triangle. Classify each triangle by the lengths of the sides.

5. 3 cm, 3 cm, 3 cm   **6.** 2.5 cm, 4.5 cm, 4.5 cm   **7.** 2.5 cm, 3 cm, 4 cm

---

MIXED APPLICATIONS

8. In a right triangle, one of the acute angles measures 40° more than the other. What is the measure of each acute angle?

_____

9. Complete: Two sides of a triangle measure 5 cm and 9 cm. The third side must be greater than 4 cm long and

less than _____ cm long.

VISUAL THINKING

10. Connect dots to draw a triangle congruent to the given triangle. (HINT: There are three different ways to draw the triangle.)

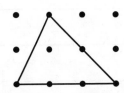

Geometric Drawings

1. On a separate piece of paper, draw a triangle that has side lengths of 3 cm and 6 cm with an included angle of 120°. Determine whether the given information makes a unique triangle, more than one triangle, or no triangle.

_____

_____

2. Determine whether the given side lengths can be used to form one unique triangle, more than one triangle, or no triangle.

	Construction 1	Construction 2	Construction 3	Construction 4
Side 1 (units)	5	8	20	1
Side 2 (units)	5	9	20	1
Side 3 (units)	10	10	20	7
Triangle Formation?				

For Exercises 3 and 4, on a separate piece of paper, draw a triangle that has degrees of 30°, 60°, and 90°. Measure the side lengths.

3. Can you draw another triangle with the same angles but different side lengths?

_____

_____

4. If you are given 3 angles in one triangle, will the triangle be unique?

_____

_____

5. Draw a freehand sketch of a triangle with three angles
that have the same measure. Explain how you made
your drawing.

_____

_____

_____

Name _____ Date _____

Ratios and Rates

Write the ratio in the form of $\frac{a}{b}$.

1. 4:9 _____ **2.** 12 to 17_____ **3.** 5 out of 8 _____ **4.** 53:100 _____

Write the ratio in simplest form.

5. $\frac{15}{35}$ _____ **6.** $\frac{12}{20}$ _____ **7.** $\frac{16}{30}$ _____ **8.** $\frac{25}{100}$ _____

Tell whether the ratio is equivalent to $\frac{2}{5}$. Write *yes* or *no*.

9. 4:10 _____ **10.** 6:12 _____ **11.** 10 to 25 _____ **12.** 50 to 20 _____

Write = or ≠.

13. $\frac{3}{6} \bigcirc \frac{1}{2}$ **14.** $\frac{4}{16} \bigcirc \frac{12}{46}$ **15.** $\frac{8}{14} \bigcirc \frac{4}{9}$ **16.** $\frac{45}{135} \bigcirc \frac{9}{27}$

17. $\frac{20}{25} \bigcirc \frac{15}{20}$ **18.** $\frac{32}{42} \bigcirc \frac{17}{21}$ **19.** $\frac{40}{50} \bigcirc \frac{4}{5}$ **20.** $\frac{6}{5} \bigcirc \frac{18}{15}$

Write the unit rate.

21. $\frac{\$1.00}{10 \text{ apples}}$ _____ **22.** $\frac{\$1.50}{30 \text{ oz of cereal}}$ _____ **23.** $\frac{\$52}{4 \text{ dinners}}$ _____

MIXED APPLICATIONS

24. Ana mixes concentrated shampoo and water in a 1:4 ratio. How many ounces of water does she mix with 4 oz of shampoo?

_____

25. Last year 66 people attended a computer workshop. This year 204 people attended. What is the ratio of last year's attendance to this year's? Write the ratio in simplest form.

_____

VISUAL THINKING

Without counting all the sections, write the ratio of the shaded area to the total area. Write the ratio as $\frac{a}{b}$ in simplest form.

26.

_____

27.

_____

28.

_____

Exploring Proportions

Write the cross products.

1. $\dfrac{14}{28} = \dfrac{1}{2}$

   $14 \times 2 =$ _____

   $28 \times 1 =$ _____

   Does $28 \times 1 = 14 \times 2$?

   _____

2. $\dfrac{1}{2} = \dfrac{8}{12}$

   $2 \times 8 =$ _____

   $1 \times 12 =$ _____

   Does $1 \times 12 = 2 \times 8$?

   _____

3. Do the ratios in Exercise 1 form a proportion? Explain your answer.

   _____

4. Do the ratios in Exercise 2 form a proportion? Explain your answer.

   _____

Write an equation that shows that the cross products are equal.

5. $\dfrac{y}{5} = \dfrac{4}{10}$ _____

6. $\dfrac{24}{18} = \dfrac{4}{n}$ _____

7. What would you do to solve the equations in Exercises 5 and 6?

   _____

   _____

Write the cross products.

8. $\dfrac{4}{1} = \dfrac{8}{2}$

9. $\dfrac{4}{5} = \dfrac{12}{15}$

10. $\dfrac{1}{6} = \dfrac{y}{18}$

11. $\dfrac{8}{x} = \dfrac{12}{9}$

_____ _____ _____ _____

Tell whether the ratios make a proportion. Write *yes* or *no*.

12. $\dfrac{4}{7}; \dfrac{12}{21}$ _____

13. 1:6; 4:24 _____

14. $\dfrac{6}{7}; \dfrac{18}{28}$ _____

15. 9:6; 12:8 _____

16. $\dfrac{2}{6}; \dfrac{40}{100}$ _____

17. $\dfrac{5}{6}; \dfrac{15}{18}$ _____

18. 1:4; 8:32 _____

19. $\dfrac{2}{10}; \dfrac{2}{20}$ _____

LOGICAL REASONING

20. In a painting, the ratio of tall buildings to short buildings is 5:4.
    In the same painting, the ratio of tall buildings to trees is 10:3.
    What is the ratio of short buildings to trees?   _____

46

Solving Proportions

Solve each proportion.

1. $\frac{2}{18} = \frac{x}{36}$ _____

2. $\frac{7}{9} = \frac{63}{c}$ _____

3. $\frac{k}{3} = \frac{15}{18}$ _____

4. $\frac{7}{a} = \frac{14}{16}$ _____

5. $\frac{1}{4} = \frac{5}{y}$ _____

6. $\frac{h}{9} = \frac{64}{72}$ _____

7. $\frac{3}{5} = \frac{z}{20}$ _____

8. $\frac{d}{9} = \frac{4}{18}$ _____

9. $\frac{3}{c} = \frac{18}{30}$ _____

10. $\frac{5}{n} = \frac{25}{45}$ _____

11. $\frac{7}{8} = \frac{21}{b}$ _____

12. $\frac{15}{12} = \frac{e}{4}$ _____

Find the value of *n*.

13. $4:5 = n:20$ _____

14. $7 \text{ to } 6 = n \text{ to } 18$ _____

15. $n:45 = 10:15$ _____

16. $5 \text{ to } 25 = 1 \text{ to } n$ _____

17. $8:36 = 2:n$ _____

18. $n \text{ to } 40 = 3 \text{ to } 8$ _____

19. $3:n = 6:15$ _____

20. $10 \text{ to } n = 5 \text{ to } 6$ _____

Solve each proportion for *x*. Let *a* = 4, *b* = 3, and *c* = 2.

21. $\frac{a}{x} = \frac{b}{c}$ _____

22. $\frac{2c}{3a} = \frac{b}{x}$ _____

23. $\frac{a + 3b}{2c} = \frac{x}{ab}$ _____

MIXED APPLICATIONS

24. Joan can paint 2 rooms of the same size in 5 hours. If she paints for $7\frac{1}{2}$ hours, how many rooms of the same size can she paint?

_____

25. The ratio of boys to girls in a science class is 8:7. If there are 14 girls, how many boys are in the class?

_____

LOGICAL REASONING

26. What fraction is equivalent to $\frac{4}{8}$ and has a numerator that is five less than three times the denominator?

_____

Proportional Tables and Equations

For Exercises 1–4, tell whether the relationship is a proportional relationship. If so, give the constant of proportionality.

1.

Number of Minutes	3	4	5	6	7
Number of Seconds	180	240	300	360	420

_____

2.

Time (h)	1	2	3	4	5
Biking Distance (mi)	12	26	36	44	50

_____

3. Naomi reads 9 pages in 27 minutes, 12 pages in 36 minutes, 15 pages in 45 minutes, and 50 pages in 150 minutes.

_____

4. A scuba diver descends at a constant rate of 8 feet per minute.

_____

For Exercises 5–8, write an equation for each relationship. Tell what the variables represent.

5. It takes Li 1 hour to drive 65 miles, 2 hours to drive 130 miles, and 3 hours to drive 195 miles.

_____

6. There are 3.9 milligrams of calcium in each ounce of cooked chicken.

_____

7.

Gallons of Gasoline	3	4	5	6
Total Cost ($)	9.45	12.60	15.75	18.90

_____

8.

Cups of Batter	2	6	8	12
Number of Muffins	5	15	20	30

_____

MIXED APPLICATIONS

Use the information on three car rental companies to solve Exercises 9 and 10.

9. Write an equation that gives the cost ,y, of renting a car for x days from Rent-All.

_____

10. What is the cost per day of renting a car from A-1?

_____

Rent-All			
Days	3	4	5	6
Total Cost ($)	55.50	74.00	92.50	111.00

A-1 Rentals	Car Town
The cost y of renting a car for x days is given by $y = 22.5x$.	The cost of renting a car from us is just $19.25 per day!

48

Proportional Relationships and Graphs

Complete each table for Exercises 1 and 2. Tell whether each relationship is a proportional relationship. Explain why or why not.

1. A student reads 65 pages per hour.

Time (h)	3	5		10
Pages			585	

2. A babysitter makes $7.50 per hour.

Time (h)	2		5	
Earnings		22.50		60

_____

_____

For Exercises 3 and 4, tell whether the relationship is a proportional relationship. Explain why or why not.

3.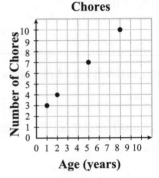

_____

4.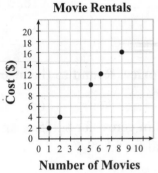

_____

5. A train travels at 72 miles per hour. Will the graph of the train's rate of speed show that the relationship between the number of miles traveled and the number of hours is a proportional relationship? Explain.

_____

Use this graph showing the relationship between time and the distance run by two people for Exercises 6–9.

6. How long does it take each person to run 1 mile?

_____

7. What does the point (0, 0) represent?

_____

8. Write an equation for the relationship between time and distance.

_____

9. Draw a line on the graph representing someone who is faster than either of these runners.

Consumer Applications

UNIT PRICE

Use a proportion to find each unit price.

1. 5 for $1.55

_____

2. 4 for $1.76

_____

3. 9 for 54¢

_____

4. 12 for $13.32

_____

5. 11 for 99¢

_____

6. 7 for $1.61

_____

7. 4 for $5.00

_____

8. 5 for $67

_____

9. 3 for 96¢

_____

Find each unit price. Round to the nearest cent when necessary. Then tell which choice has the lower unit price.

10. a 12-oz box of cereal for $2.55 or an 18-oz box of cereal for $3.29

_____

11. a 5-lb bag of grapefruit for $2.99 or an 8-lb bag of grapefruit for $5.25

_____

12. two paintbrushes for 59¢ or 5 paintbrushes for $1.29

_____

13. a package of 3 pairs of socks for $5.98 or a package of 8 pairs for $14.79

_____

MIXED APPLICATIONS

14. Anne is shopping for notebooks. Which is a better buy: 3 for $3.29 or 2 for $2.89?

_____

15. About how long is the curved edge of $\frac{1}{4}$ of a 12-inch pizza? Round your answer to the nearest tenth of an inch. Hint: C = πd and π = 3.14.

_____

EVERYDAY MATH CONNECTION

16. Jeremy bought the following groceries: 5 lb of apples for $1.89, 8 lb of grapefruit for $4.88, 5 lb of potatoes for $0.99, and a 12-oz head of lettuce for 89¢. What is the unit price of each item?

apples: _____   grapefruit: _____   potatoes: _____   lettuce: _____

Unit Rates

1. Brandon enters bike races. He bikes $8\frac{1}{2}$ miles every $\frac{1}{2}$ hour. Complete the table to find how far Brandon bikes for each time interval.

Distance (mi)	$8\frac{1}{2}$				
Time (h)	$\frac{1}{2}$	1	$1\frac{1}{2}$	2	$2\frac{1}{2}$

Simplify each complex fraction.

2. $\dfrac{\frac{3}{4}}{\frac{2}{3}} =$ _____

3. $\dfrac{\frac{1}{2}}{\frac{5}{8}} =$ _____

4. $\dfrac{\frac{4}{5}}{\frac{2}{3}} =$ _____

5. $\dfrac{\frac{6}{7}}{\frac{1}{7}} =$ _____

Find each unit rate.

6. Julio walks $3\frac{1}{2}$ miles in $1\frac{1}{4}$ hours.

_____

7. Kenny reads $\frac{5}{8}$ page in $\frac{2}{3}$ minute.

_____

8. Marcia uses $\frac{3}{4}$ cup sugar when she halves the recipe.

_____

9. Sandra tiles $\frac{5}{4}$ square yards in $\frac{1}{3}$ hour.

_____

Use the information for two cell phone companies to solve Exercises 10–14.

10. What is the unit rate for On Call?

_____

11. What is the unit rate for Talk Time?

_____

On Call	Talk Time
3.5 hours: $10	$\frac{1}{2}$ hour: $1.25

12. Determine which of the companies offers the best deal. Explain your answer.

_____

13. Another company offers a rate of $0.05 per minute. How would you find the unit rate per hour?

_____

14. Is the company in Exercise 13 a better deal than On Call or Talk Time?

_____

Understanding Scale Drawings

The scale of a room in a blueprint is 3 in:5 ft. A wall in the same blueprint is 18 in.

Blueprint length (in.)	3	6	9	12	18
Actual length (ft)					

1. Complete the table.

2. How long is the actual wall? _____

3. A window in the room has an actual width of 2.5 feet. Find the width of the window in the blueprint.

_____

4. The scale in the drawing is 2 in.:4 ft. What are the length and width of the actual room? Find the area of the actual room.

_____

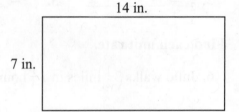

5. The scale in the drawing is 2 cm:5 m. What are the length and width of the actual room? Find the area of the actual room.

_____

_____

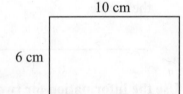

In the scale drawing below, assume the rectangle is drawn on centimeter grid paper. The scale is 1 cm:4 m.

6. Redraw the rectangle on centimeter grid paper using a scale of 1 cm:6 m.

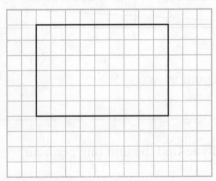   

7. What are the actual length and width of the rectangle using the original scale? What are the actual dimensions using the new scale?

_____

Exploring Scale Drawings

Use the scale drawing of the community recreation center. Write the proportion you can use to find actual dimensions. Round measurements to the nearest cm.

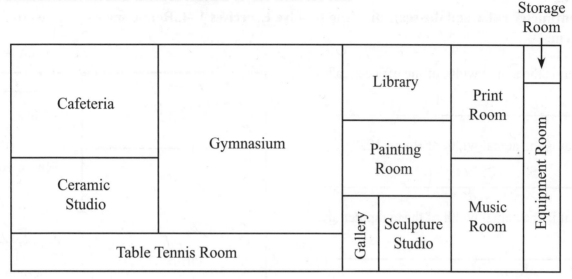

Scale: 1 cm = 6 m

1. length of the gymnasium

_____

2. length of the library

_____

3. length of the ceramic studio

_____

4. width of the library

_____

5. width of the painting room

_____

6. width of the cafeteria

_____

Make a scale drawing to enlarge each shape to twice its size.

7.

8.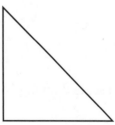

WRITER'S CORNER

9. Explain how you would make a scale drawing of a room in your home.

_____

Problem Solving

USE A SCALE DRAWING

Use a centimeter ruler and the scale drawing to solve Exercises 1–4. Round measurements to the nearest cm.

Scale: 1 cm = 6 ft

1. What is the actual width of the office area?

   _____

2. What is the actual width of Room 103?

   _____

3. What is the actual width of the computer area?

   _____

4. What are the actual length and width of Room 101?

   _____

Room 101

Closet

Room 105

Office Area

Computer

Room 103

MIXED APPLICATIONS

5. Mrs. Chang uses $1\frac{1}{4}$ yd of fabric to make a square pillow. How much fabric will she need to make 5 square pillows?

   _____

6. Diane wants to order a new door for the closet. What is the width of the new door? Use the scale drawing above.

   _____

WRITER'S CORNER

7. Write a problem in which a scale drawing is used.

   _____

   _____

54

Scale Drawings

Use the scale of 1 cm:15 cm to find each missing dimension.

1. drawing: 4 cm

actual: _____ cm

2. drawing: 9 cm

actual: _____ cm

3. drawing: 22.5 cm

actual: _____ cm

Use the scale of 15 cm:1 cm to find the missing dimension.

4. drawing: 75 cm

actual _____ cm

5. drawing: _____ cm

actual 12.4 cm

6. drawing: 39 cm

actual: _____ cm

Eartha completed a scale drawing of her school. Her scale was 1 in.:60 ft. Measure the drawing to the nearest $\frac{1}{4}$. Then use the scale to find the actual dimensions. Write both the drawing dimensions and the actual dimensions.

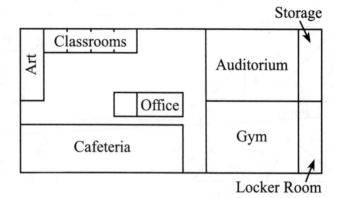

7. length of the entire school

_____

8. length of the cafeteria

_____

MIXED APPLICATIONS

Solve. Use the scale of 1 in:50 ft.

9. The dimensions of a scale drawing of a library are 4 in. by 2 in. What are the actual dimensions of the library?

_____

10. A concrete walkway is being installed around the perimeter of the library in Exercise 9. Each concrete slab is 10 ft by 10 ft. How many concrete slabs are needed?

_____

VISUAL THINKING

11. Use the scale of 1 cm:1.5 m to make a scale drawing of a rectangle 9 m by 21 m.

_____

55

Similar Figures

Each pair of figures is similar. Find x.

1.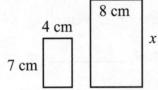

_____

2.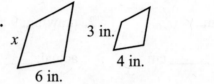

_____

3.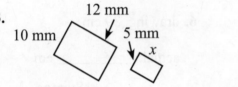

_____

4.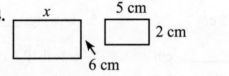

_____

5.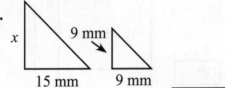

_____

6.

_____

7.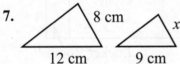

_____

8.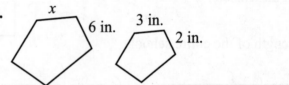

_____

MIXED APPLICATIONS

9. The length and width of a rectangular box are 10 in. and 8 in., respectively. Another rectangular box has a length of 15 in. and a width of 12 in., respectively. Are the length and width dimensions of the two rectangular boxes similar?

_____

10. Mrs. Nahamura bought 2.5 lb of fish filets for $5.50. What was the unit price of the fish filets?

_____

MIXED REVIEW

Estimate.

11. $\frac{5}{6} + 1\frac{6}{7}$ _____

12. $2\frac{3}{5} - 1\frac{1}{2}$ _____

13. $\frac{4}{5} \times 39$ _____

14. $15\frac{1}{8} \div 3\frac{1}{4}$ _____

Indirect Measurement

Each pair of triangles is similar. Find *x*.

1.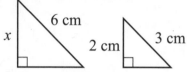

_____

2.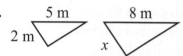

_____

3.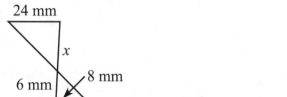

_____

4.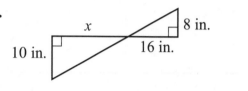

_____

5.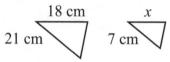

_____

6.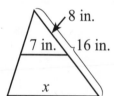

_____

MIXED APPLICATIONS

7. A building casts a shadow that is 32 ft long
at the same time a person 6 ft tall walking
in front of the building casts an 8 ft shadow.
What is the height of the building?

_____

8. Miyo has $1.25 in dimes and quarters. If
one of the dimes were a quarter, she would
have $1.40. How many dimes and how
many quarters does Miyo have?

_____

NUMBER SENSE • MENTAL MATH

9. The sides of two triangles are in the ratio of 2:1. If the lengths of the sides of the first triangle are
5 cm, 9 cm, and 11 cm, what are the lengths of the sides of the second triangle?

_____

10. If the ratio of the triangles in Exercise 9 is reversed to 1:2, what will be the lengths of the sides of
the second triangle?

_____

© Houghton Mifflin Harcourt Publishing Company

Proportion in Angles and Sides

Solve.

1. A person 5 feet tall casts a shadow 3 feet long. A nearby tree casts a shadow 15 feet long. How tall is the tree?

   _____

2. Triangles *XYZ* and *MNO* are similar. Find the length of *MO*.

   _____

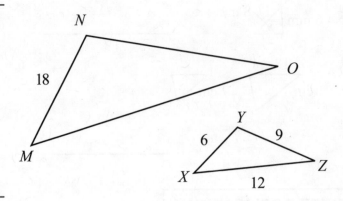

3. When a pole 20 feet tall casts a shadow 15 feet long, how tall is a nearby tree that casts a shadow 24 feet long?

   _____

4. Triangles *QRS* and *JKL* are similar. Find the length of *QR*.

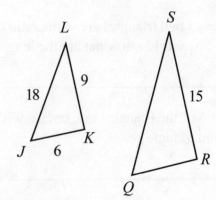

   _____

Connecting Percents and Decimals

Use the grid to shade each amount.

1. 30%   **2.** 0.5   **3.** 65%   **4.** 73%

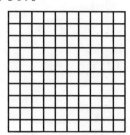 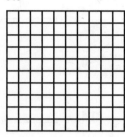 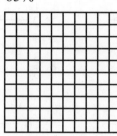 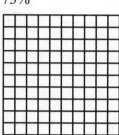

Write the decimal as a percent.

5. 0.46 _____   **6.** 0.37 _____   **7.** 0.17 _____   **8.** 0.23 _____

9. 0.2 _____   **10.** 0.8 _____   **11.** 0.07 _____   **12.** 1.33 _____

13. 0.01 _____   **14.** 0.3 _____   **15.** 2.07 _____   **16.** 8.10 _____

Write the percent as a decimal.

17. 19% _____   **18.** 46% _____   **19.** 2% _____   **20.** 170% _____

21. 8% _____   **22.** 89% _____   **23.** 140% _____   **24.** 4% _____

25. 31% _____   **26.** 150% _____   **27.** 11% _____   **28.** 3% _____

MIXED APPLICATIONS

29. Shada has 100 pieces of colored paper. Ninety-four of these are blue. What percent of the pieces of paper are blue?

_____

30. A restaurant has 100 seats. If $\frac{4}{5}$ of the seats are occupied, how many of the seats are unoccupied?

_____

NUMBER SENSE

31. In a survey, 48% of the people questioned said they watch sports on television. Were there more people who said they watch sports or more who said they do not?

_____

59

Connecting Percents and Fractions

Write each fraction as a percent.

1. $\frac{3}{10}$ _____   2. $\frac{2}{5}$ _____   3. $\frac{1}{2}$ _____   4. $\frac{1}{10}$ _____   5. $\frac{1}{4}$ _____

6. $\frac{11}{20}$ _____   7. $\frac{3}{25}$ _____   8. $\frac{3}{5}$ _____   9. $\frac{3}{4}$ _____   10. $\frac{7}{20}$ _____

11. $\frac{7}{10}$ _____   12. $\frac{3}{20}$ _____   13. $\frac{9}{10}$ _____   14. $\frac{4}{5}$ _____   15. $\frac{10}{25}$ _____

Write each percent as a fraction in simplest form.

16. 30% _____   17. 18% _____   18. 45% _____   19. 28% _____   20. 85% _____

21. 96% _____   22. 39% _____   23. 78% _____   24. 44% _____   25. 65% _____

26. 34% _____   27. 76% _____   28. 88% _____   29. 12% _____   30. 56% _____

31. 24% _____   32. 63% _____   33. 11% _____   34. 42% _____   35. 60% _____

36. 54% _____   37. 92% _____   38. 86% _____   39. 14% _____   40. 4% _____

MIXED APPLICATIONS

41. Mrs. Molina asked her students what they do after school. She found that $\frac{3}{4}$ of her students do their homework. What percent of her students do their homework after school?

_____

42. A tree was 2 yards tall when it was planted. It is now 4 yards 2 feet tall. How many feet has the tree grown?

_____

SCIENCE CONNECTION

43. A kernel of wheat is 14.5% bran and 2.5% germ. Write each percent as a fraction in simplest form.

_____

Finding the Percent One Number Is of Another

Solve. You may use either the proportion method or the equation method.

1. What percent of 55 is 22?

_____

2. What percent of 48 is 12?

_____

3. 17 is what percent of 50?

_____

4. 18 is what percent of 60?

_____

5. What percent of 50 is 34?

_____

6. What percent of 25 is 18?

_____

7. 15 is what percent of 75?

_____

8. 30 is what percent of 60?

_____

9. What percent of 45 is 25?

_____

10. What percent of 75 is 45?

_____

11. 30 is what percent of 120?

_____

12. 18 is what percent of 90?

_____

MIXED APPLICATIONS

13. Joe earned $2,400 this year. Last year he earned $1,800. This year's earnings were what percentage of last year's?

_____

14. Dolores bought 3 tapes that cost $4.95 each. The tax on her purchase was 6%. What was her total bill?

_____

MIXED REVIEW

Solve each equation. Check your solutions.

15. $x + 3.1 = 5$ _____

16. $0.9z = 10.8$ _____

17. $c - 0.34 = 2.19$ _____

18. $\dfrac{b}{0.05} = 5.3$ _____

61

Consumer Applications of Percent

Find the amount of discount at 30% off. Round to the nearest cent when necessary.

1. $7.00 _____
2. $110.50 _____
3. $99.00 _____

4. $65.00 _____
5. $78.50 _____
6. $240.00 _____

Find the amount of sales tax if the rate is 6%. Round to the nearest cent when necessary.

7. $8.00 _____
8. $112.50 _____
9. $92.00 _____

10. $65.00 _____
11. $80.25 _____
12. $235.00 _____

Find the sale price at 15% off. Round to the nearest cent when necessary.

13. $80.00 _____
14. $24.50 _____
15. $295.00 _____

16. $52.75 _____
17. $18.00 _____
18. $500.00 _____

Find each total cost if the sales tax rate is 7%. Round to the nearest cent when necessary.

19. $12.00 _____
20. $8.95 _____
21. $15.50 _____

MIXED APPLICATIONS

22. Glowmart marked down its stock 32%. What will be the sale price of a $60 jacket?

_____

23. What is the total cost of a $28 pair of jeans if the sales tax is 7.5%?

_____

WRITER'S CORNER

24. Write and solve a word problem involving a $145.00 price and a 5.5% sales tax.

_____

Exploring Percent Problems

Use coins to model each type of percent problem.

1. Line up 10 coins so all of them show *heads*. You want to turn over 40% of them to show *tails*. Write a proportion to determine the number of coins showing *tails*. **Think:** 40 is to 100 as what number is to 10?

_____

2. Line up 10 coins so that 3 show *heads* and 7 show *tails*. Write an equation to determine what percent show *tails*. **Think:** What percent of 10 is 7?

_____

3. Line up only 4 coins. Move the remaining 6 to the side. The 4 coins represent 40% of the total coins. Write an equation to determine the total number of coins. **Think:** 40% of what number is 4?

_____

Choose the correct equation or proportion for each problem. Circle *a*, *b*, or *c*.

4. Of 32 cars, 8 were sold. What percent were sold?

   a. $n\% \times 8 = 32$ **b.** $n\% \times 32 = 8$ **c.** $n = 8\%$ of 32

5. Ryan is saving 40% of his allowance. Each week he receives $5. How much does he save each week?

   a. $\dfrac{40}{100} = \dfrac{n}{5}$ **b.** $\dfrac{40}{n} = \dfrac{5}{100}$ **c.** $\dfrac{40}{100} = \dfrac{5}{n}$

6. Maria sold 21 items. This is 30% of the total number she needs to sell. How many items must Maria sell?

   a. $21 \times n = 30\%$ **b.** $n = 30\% \times 21$ **c.** $30\% \times n = 21$

NUMBER SENSE

7. Out of 250 items for sale, 25 are marked down. What percent of the items are not marked down?

_____

Exploring Percent of Increase and Decrease

1. In 1990 an automobile dealer sold 800 new
   cars. In 1991 the dealer sold 600 new cars.
   What is the percent of decrease?

   Think: amount of decrease is 800 − _____ = _____

   Percent of decrease = $\dfrac{\text{amount of decrease}}{\text{original amount}}$ = $\dfrac{\boxed{}}{800}$

   Percent of decrease = $\dfrac{1}{\boxed{}}$ = _____%

Solve.

2. Find the percent of increase if the amount
   of increase is 80 and the original amount
   is 100.

   _____

3. Find the percent of decrease if the amount
   of decrease is 36 and the original amount
   is 40.

   _____

4. Find the percent of decrease if the amount
   of decrease is $100 and the original salary
   is $25,000.

   _____

5. In 1990, there were 20 convenience stores
   in a city. By 1991, there were 60 convenience
   stores in the city. What is the percent increase?

   _____

LOGICAL REASONING

6. Windle County had 4,000 high school students in 1990
   and 4,500 high school students in 2000. By 2010 the
   number of high school students had increased 50% over
   the 1990 number. How many more high school students
   did the county have in 2010 than in 2000?

_____

Percent of Increase and Decrease

Find each percent of increase or decrease.

1. 2000 cost: $60
2001 cost: $80

_____

2. 1990 earnings: $30,000
2000 earnings: $45,000

_____

3. 2009 amount: 600
2011 amount: 360

_____

4. 2000 sales: 500
2010 sales: 1,000

_____

5. 2010 savings: $4,000
2011 savings: $1,500

_____

6. 1999 amount: 1,450
2001 amount: 1,305

_____

7. 2011 cost: $12,000
2012 cost: $16,000

_____

8. 2005 sales: 90
2010 sales: 72

_____

9. 2009 amount: 200
2010 amount: 230

_____

10. 1990 cost: $25.00
1991 cost: $25.50

_____

11. 2009 sales: 390
2011 sales: 273

_____

12. 2000 earnings: $1,580
2010 earnings: $1,738

_____

MIXED APPLICATIONS

13. Last year Cindy built a gymnastics set for $50. This year it cost her $75 to build one. What is the percent of increase?

_____

14. Last week an almanac cost $3.50. This week it is on sale for $2.80. What is the percent decrease?

_____

EVERYDAY MATH CONNECTION

Discount is the amount off the regular price of an item. Discount is often written as a percent of the regular price. The sale price is the difference between the regular price and the amount of discount.

The regular price of a car is $9,872. The car is on sale at a 15% discount.

15. What is the amount of discount?

_____

16. What is the sale price?

_____

Simple Interest

Find each interest using the formula *I = prt*.

1. $p = \$625$
$r = 6\%$ per year
$t = 2$ yr

$I =$ _____

2. $p = \$150$
$r = 8\%$ per year
$t = 2$ yr

$I =$ _____

3. $p = \$225$
$r = 5\%$ per year
$t = 3$ yr

$I =$ _____

4. $p = \$1,590$
$r = 7\%$ per year
$t = 4$ yr

$I =$ _____

5. $p = \$1,940$
$r = 3\%$ per year
$t = 1\frac{1}{2}$ yr

$I =$ _____

6. $p = \$630$
$r = 4\%$ per year
$t = 3$ yr

$I =$ _____

7. $p = \$450$
$r = 7\%$ per year
$t = 4$ yr

$I =$ _____

8. $p = \$940$
$r = 8\%$ per year
$t = 3$ mo

$I =$ _____

9. $p = \$380$
$r = 7\%$ per year
$t = 6$ mo

$I =$ _____

10. $p = \$1,050$
$r = 2\%$ per year
$t = 1\frac{1}{2}$ yr

$I =$ _____

11. $p = \$800$
$r = 6\%$ per year
$t = 1$ yr

$I =$ _____

12. $p = \$1,100$
$r = 3\%$ per year
$t = 9$ mo

$I =$ _____

MIXED APPLICATIONS

13. Tina borrows $4,000 for 2 yr. The bank charges 12% interest per year. How much interest must she pay? Find the total amount she must pay.

_____

14. Ellis borrows $750 to buy a piano. The bank charges 8% interest per year. He will pay $30 in interest. For how long does Ellis borrow the money?

_____

MIXED REVIEW

Estimate the number.

15. 11% of what number is 91?

_____

16. 25% of what number is 24?

_____

Estimate the percent.

17. $\frac{48}{98}$ _____

18. 31:120 _____

19. $\frac{110}{532}$ _____

Adding Integers on a Number Line

Use a number line to find each sum.

1. 4 + -2

_____

2. -5 + 1

_____

3. -8 + 8

_____

4. -6 + 3

_____

5. 5 + -6

_____

6. 7 + -8

_____

Find each sum by using the absolute values.

7. 5 + 6 _____

8. -16 + -4 _____

9. 9 + -9 _____

10. -17 + -8 _____

11. 24 + 30 _____

12. 8 + -11 _____

13. 4 + 8 _____

14. 12 + -2 _____

15. -6 + 9 _____

16. -8 + 2 _____

17. -9 + -1 _____

18. -4 + 5 _____

19. 17 + 18 _____

20. -7 + -3 _____

21. 3 + -9 _____

22. -25 + -2 + 49 _____

23. -11 + |-2| _____

MIXED APPLICATIONS

24. The temperature at 8 P.M. was -8°C. By midnight, it had fallen two degrees. What was the temperature at midnight?

_____

25. Diana had $3\frac{1}{4}$ yd of material to make a shirt and a matching scarf. The shirt required $2\frac{2}{3}$ yd of the material. How much did she have left for the scarf?

_____

LOGICAL REASONING

26. If a and b are integers and $a + b = 0$, what do you know about the values of a and b?

_____

     Core Skills Math, Grade 7

Name _____ Date _____

Exploring Addition of Integers

Think about a thermometer.

1. If the temperature is 5 degrees above zero and then drops 7 degrees, will the final temperature be higher or lower than zero?

   _____

2. Will the final temperature be positive or negative?

3. What is 5 + -7?

   _____

4. If the temperature is 7 degrees below zero and then rises 3 degrees, will the final temperature be positive or negative?

   _____

5. What is -7 + 3?

   _____

Find each sum. You may use a number line.

6. 5 + 2 _____   7. 10 + 8 _____   8. -12 + -12 _____   9. -11 + -8 _____

10. -8 + 4 _____   11. 10 + -5 _____   12. -9 + 5 _____   13. -4 + 11 _____

14. -8 + -2 _____   15. -9 + 19 _____   16. 16 + 8 _____   17. -14 + 10 _____

18. 15 + -5 _____   19. 7 + 11 _____   20. -8 + 8 _____   21. -17 + 12 _____

MIXED REVIEW

Find each product or quotient.

22. $4 \times \frac{1}{4}$ _____

23. $\frac{6}{7} \div \frac{1}{14}$ _____

24. $2\frac{1}{2} \times 3\frac{3}{10}$ _____

25. $1\frac{5}{9} \div 2\frac{1}{3}$ _____

26. $1\frac{5}{6} \times \frac{8}{3}$ _____

27. $4\frac{3}{4} \div 1\frac{3}{16}$ _____

Find the area of each figure.

28.

2 in.

5 in.

29.

4 m

5 m

30.

2 cm

2 cm

31.

4 m

_____   _____

Adding Integers

Find each sum.

1. 4 + 3 _____

2. -2 + -5 _____

3. -9 + 4 _____

4. 7 + -2 _____

5. -11 + 4 _____

6. -4 + -4 _____

7. 6 + -3 _____

8. 3 + -12 _____

9. 5 + -3 _____

10. 12 + -20 _____

11. 15 + -4 _____

12. 40 + 5 _____

13. -2 + 22 _____

14. -7 + 7 _____

15. 13 + -3 _____

16. 25 + -33 _____

17. -19 + -4 _____

18. 12 + -9 _____

19. -21 + 21 _____

20. -4 + 20 _____

21. 60 + -8 _____

22. -6 + 22 _____

23. -23 + -16 _____

24. 43 + -26 _____

25. 126 + -9 _____

26. -102 + 88 _____

27. 28 + -97 _____

28. -154 + 6 _____

29. 7 + -3 + 11 _____

30. 22 + -5 + -2 _____

31. -18 + 4 + -24 _____

32. (4 + -16) + 12 _____

33. (-52 + 21) + 25 _____

34. 9 + (6 + -14) _____

MIXED APPLICATIONS

35. A diver is swimming at -10 m. He then descends 3 m and rises 6 m. At what new level is the diver swimming?

_____

36. Yesterday $37\frac{1}{2}$% of the customers in Mall Mart paid by credit card. If 582 customers paid by credit card, how many customers were there in all?

_____

37. Each term in a number sequence is 5 greater than the term before it. The first term is -24. Write the next six terms in the sequence.

_____

38. The level of water in a pail has changed by -7 in. from the original water level. If the original level was 23 in., what is the current level?

_____

NUMBER SENSE

39. The sum of two integers is -23. If the sign of one integer is changed, the new sum will be -3. What are the two integers? Which integer will have its sign changed?

_____

69

Name _____ Date _____

Exploring Integer Subtraction

Use circles and squares to model equations. Let ■ represent 1 and ● represent -1.

1. Model the equation 4 + -2 = ☐.

Your model must have _____ ●

and _____ ■. Since _____

unpaired ■ remain, 4 + -2 = _____.

2. Model the equation -2 + 4 = ☐.

Since there are _____ unpaired ■,

-2 + 4 = _____.

3. Compare the equations

4 + -2 = _____ and -2 + 4 = _____

_____ = _____

Solve each subtraction equation.

4. -3 − -7 = _____   **5.** -3 − 7 = _____   **6.** 3 − -7 = _____

Rewrite each expression as an addition expression and solve.

7. 6 − 8 _____   **8.** -8 − -6 _____   **9.** 8 − -6 _____

VISUAL THINKING

10. Let ■ represent 1 and ● represent -1.
Use the figure to solve 3 − 7.

_____

Subtracting Integers Using Models

1. Tell which model to use to answer $-4 - 2$. _____

a.    b. 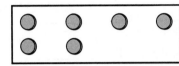   c.

2. The model shows -3. How can you find $-3 - 1$ using counters?

_____

_____

Find each difference.

3. $-8 - -3$ _____   **4.** $-7 - -6$ _____   **5.** $-6 - 4$ _____

Complete each of the following.

6. $8 - -5 = 8 +$ _____   **7.** $-9 - -5 = -9 +$ _____

8. $-4 - 1 = -4 +$ _____   **9.** $9 - 4 = 9 +$ _____

Rewrite each subtraction expression as an addition expression. Solve.

10. $-6 - -12$ _____   **11.** $-8 - 6$ _____   **12.** $12 - 5$ _____

13. $19 - 9$ _____   **14.** $-6 - 10$ _____   **15.** $7 - -5$ _____

WRITER'S CORNER

16. Write two problems requiring subtraction of integers to solve.

_____

_____

_____

_____

Subtracting Integers

Find each difference.

1. $13 - 9$ _____

2. $0 - -6$ _____

3. $4 - 9$ _____

4. $6 - -9$ _____

5. $15 - -4$ _____

6. $8 - -6$ _____

7. $0 - 7$ _____

8. $12 - -12$ _____

9. $-9 - -15$ _____

10. $-6 - -10$ _____

11. $8 - 12$ _____

12. $-15 - -9$ _____

13. $14 - 9$ _____

14. $-17 - -12$ _____

15. $-9 - -8$ _____

16. $-11 - -5$ _____

17. $-13 - -5$ _____

18. $-6 - -8$ _____

19. $-15 - -2$ _____

20. $5 - 5$ _____

21. $-8 - -8$ _____

MIXED APPLICATIONS

22. The average temperature for the week of January 7–14 was -16°C. The average temperature for the week of January 15–22 was 3°C. What is the absolute value of the difference between these two temperatures?

_____

23. Kareem bought a new collar and a toy mouse for his cat. The collar cost $3.50, the toy mouse cost $2.70, and the tax was 5%. How much change did Kareem get from a $10 bill?

_____

MATH CONNECTION

Find each difference. Use a calculator that has a $\boxed{+/-}$ key.

Examples

A. $25 - 19$

$25 \boxed{-} 19 \boxed{=} \boxed{ 6}$

B. $121 - 253$

$121 \boxed{-} 253 \boxed{=} \boxed{ -132}$

C. $-22 - 19$

$22 \boxed{+/-} \boxed{-} 19 \boxed{=} \boxed{ -41}$

D. $-88 - -119$

$88 \boxed{+/-} \boxed{-} 119 \boxed{+/-} \boxed{=} \boxed{ 31}$

24. $251 - 352$ _____

25. $759 - 640$ _____

26. $5,239 - 5,821$ _____

27. $264 - 199$ _____

More Subtracting Integers

Find each difference.

1. 4 − -13 _____

2. -3 − -11 _____

3. -17 − -11 _____

4. -8 − -2 _____

5. -32 − -54 _____

6. -30 − 12 _____

7. 22 − 14 _____

8. -7 − -12 _____

9. -14 − -30 _____

10. -33 − -22 _____

11. 41 − -22 _____

12. 28 − 42 _____

13. 32 − 24 _____

14. 100 − -2 _____

15. -16 − 6 _____

16. -3 − -3 _____

17. 11 − -20 _____

18. -74 − 44 _____

19. 126 − 154 _____

20. -25 − -41 _____

21. -41 − -44 _____

22. 7 − 35 _____

23. 61 − -61 _____

24. 24 − 24 _____

Compute.

25. -4 − -2 − 7 _____

26. -11 + 2 − 8 _____

27. (-7 + 3) − -4 _____

MIXED APPLICATIONS

28. Lian is standing 20 ft above sea level. Mary is swimming 10 ft below sea level, or at -10 ft. How much higher is Lian's position than Mary's?

_____

29. A diver is at -20 m. The ocean floor is at -135 m. If the diver rises 3 m, how far will she be from the ocean floor?

_____

30. The sum of two integers is -9. When the smaller integer is subtracted from the larger integer, the difference is 1. What are the integers?

_____

31. At Multi Muffins, $\frac{1}{3}$ of the muffins sold are bran muffins. Of the bran muffins sold, $\frac{2}{5}$ contain raisins. What fraction of the muffins sold are raisin bran muffins?

_____

MIXED REVIEW

Compare. Write <, >, or =.

32. $\frac{4}{5} \bigcirc \frac{3}{8}$

33. $3\frac{1}{4} \bigcirc 3\frac{3}{10}$

34. $\frac{7}{4} \bigcirc \frac{9}{8}$

35. $\frac{11}{7} \bigcirc 1\frac{1}{3}$

36. -10 $\bigcirc$ 3

37. -5 $\bigcirc$ -1

38. 0 $\bigcirc$ -11

39. 6 $\bigcirc$ -10

Using Integers

Find each sum or difference.

1. -10 + 14 _____

2. 13 − 15 _____

3. 4 + −13 _____

4. -15 + -11 _____

5. 20 + -14 _____

6. 17 − −9 _____

7. 15 + −25 _____

8. 16 − -4 _____

9. -25 − -19 _____

10. -11 − 5 _____

11. 30 + −8 _____

12. -13 − −7 _____

13. -17 + -2 _____

14. 26 − −9 _____

15. -21 − 8 _____

16. 32 + −7 _____

17. 4 − 8 _____

18. -5 + -5 _____

19. -8 + −3 _____

20. 9 + -2 _____

21. -10 − 5 _____

22. -12 − -11 _____

23. -9 + 4 _____

24. 12 − -16 _____

25. 8 + -5 + -1 _____

26. -7 + -4 + 2 _____

27. -4 + -8 + -11 _____

28. -4 + 5 + -15 _____

29. -10 + -14 + 12 _____

30. -15 + 14 + -11 _____

MIXED APPLICATIONS

31. The Tigers gained 8 yd in one play. In the next play they lost 12 yd. How many yards did they lose in the two plays?

_____

32. The temperature in Oslo was -16°C in the evening. It dropped 8 degrees by morning. What was the temperature in the morning?

_____

33. A share of stock dropped 6 points on Tuesday. On Wednesday, the same stock gained 3 points. What was the total loss for the two days?

_____

34. The temperature in New City was -1°C. Then it rose 7 degrees. What was the new temperature?

_____

WRITER'S CORNER

35. Write a problem about a bank account. Include one deposit and two withdrawals in your problem.

_____

_____

_____

Exploring Integer Multiplication

Complete the number line and integer addition for Exercise 1.

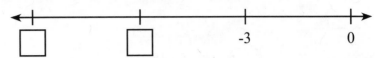

1. $3 \times -3 = \blacksquare$

   $3 \times -3 = -3 + _____ + _____ = _____$

Complete each pattern.

2. $0 \times -5 = 0$

   $1 \times -5 = -5$

   $2 \times -5 = _____$

   $3 \times -5 = _____$

   $4 \times -5 = _____$

   $5 \times -5 = _____$

3. $-15 \times 3 = -45$

   $-12 \times 3 = -36$

   $-9 \times 3 = _____$

   $-6 \times 3 = _____$

   $-3 \times 3 = _____$

   $0 \times 3 = _____$

4. $-1 \times -3 = 3$

   $-2 \times -3 = _____$

   $-3 \times -3 = _____$

   $-4 \times -3 = _____$

   $-5 \times -3 = _____$

   $-6 \times -3 = _____$

Find each product.

5. -8×-3 _____

6. -8×3 _____

7. 8×-3 _____

8. -7×-4 _____

9. -7×4 _____

10. 7×-4 _____

Find each value.

11. $(-3)^3$ _____

12. $(-3)^1$ _____

13. $(-1)^2$ _____

14. $(-4)^2 = -4 \times \_\_\_\_\_ = \_\_\_\_\_$

15. $(-5)^3 - \_\_\_\_\_ \times \_\_\_\_\_ \times \_\_\_\_\_ = \_\_\_\_\_$

LOGICAL REASONING

16. Write the next three numbers in the following pattern.

   $-64, -60, -56,$ _____, _____, _____

17. What are two ways to complete the pattern?

   _____

   _____

Name _____   Date _____

Multiplying Integers

1. 8 · 4 _____

2. 16 · -2 _____

3. -13 · 6 _____

4. -14 · 9 _____

5. 7 · -3 _____

6. -2 · 17 _____

7. 20 · -6 _____

8. -5 · 18 _____

9. -18 · -3 _____

10. 6 · -15 _____

11. -17 · -9 _____

12. 9 · -6 _____

13. 6 · 11 _____

14. 13 · -3 _____

15. -10 · -5 _____

16. 14 · -9 _____

17. -17 · 4 _____

18. -15 · -8 _____

19. 9 · -9 _____

20. 2 · -18 _____

21. -3 · -8 _____

22. -18 · -8 _____

23. 16 · -5 _____

24. 22 · -10 _____

25. 30 · -3 _____

26. -25 · -6 _____

27. 40 · -3 _____

28. -2 · -2 · 2 _____

29. 4 · -5 · -2 _____

30. -13 · 3 · -2 _____

31. -3 · 6 · 2 _____

32. -18 · 2 · -2 _____

33. 11 · -3 · 6 _____

MIXED APPLICATIONS

34. Erica has $40. She wants to buy 3 cans of blue paint for her bicycle. Paint costs $5 per can. How much money will she have left?

_____

35. The sum of two integers is -1. The product of these integers is -56. What are the integers?

_____

SCIENCE CONNECTION

36. Have you ever wondered how much food is used to produce your canned favorites in the supermarket? When food is cooked, it loses weight because water is removed. During processing, 500 pounds of a certain food loses 90 pounds of water. How many cans of prepared food are produced if each can holds 1 pound of food?

_____

Dividing Integers

Find each quotient.

1. $14 \div 2$ _____

2. $24 \div -4$ _____

3. $-36 \div 4$ _____

4. $-27 \div 3$ _____

5. $-18 \div -2$ _____

6. $121 \div -11$ _____

7. $-81 \div -9$ _____

8. $0 \div -10$ _____

9. $40 \div -8$ _____

10. $-105 \div 15$ _____

11. $28 \div 7$ _____

12. $-16 \div -16$ _____

13. $28 \div -7$ _____

14. $-32 \div -4$ _____

15. $-45 \div -5$ _____

16. $-82 \div -41$ _____

17. $25 \div -5$ _____

18. $-144 \div -4$ _____

19. $15 \div -3$ _____

20. $-32 \div 16$ _____

21. $-100 \div -25$ _____

MIXED APPLICATIONS

22. The temperatures for December 9–12 were -12°C, -6°C, 3°C, and 5°C. What is the average temperature for the four-day period?

_____

23. Computers and calculators are being sold at 25% off. Chante buys a calculator that is regularly priced at $75. How much does she pay?

_____

24. Heidi lost an average of 4 pounds a month for 5 months. What was her total weight loss?

_____

25. A car that has been getting 15 miles to a gallon of gas had a tune-up. Now it gets 18 miles a gallon. What is the percent of increase?

_____

MIXED REVIEW

Find the complement and supplement for each angle with the given measure.

26. 8° _____

27. 36° _____

28. 89° _____

29. 41° _____

30. 65° _____

31. 73° _____

More Dividing Integers

Find each quotient.

1. -22 ÷ 2 _____

2. 39 ÷ -13 _____

3. -45 ÷ 9 _____

4. -99 ÷ −3 _____

5. 84 ÷ -7 _____

6. -110 ÷ −5 _____

7. -125 ÷ 5 _____

8. 270 ÷ -9 _____

9. -42 ÷ 6 _____

10. $\dfrac{-240}{-20}$ _____

11. $\dfrac{560}{-40}$ _____

12. $\dfrac{640}{-80}$ _____

Compute.

13. (-99 ÷ 3) · 2 _____

14. -13 + (-34 ÷ -2) _____

15. 90 − (99 ÷ 9) _____

16. 12 · (39 ÷ -3) _____

17. (-86 ÷ -43) + 98 _____

18. (64 ÷ -8) · 3 _____

MIXED APPLICATIONS

19. A water tank has a leak. The amount of water changes by -8 gal per day. When the total change is -400 gal, the water pump will stop working. In how many days will this happen?

_____

20. A rope is used to repair a broken swing. During the summer, the length of the rope changes by -2 in. per week. How much shorter is the rope at the end of 12 weeks of summer?

_____

Use the following statement to solve Exercises 21–22.

If *n* is any negative integer, *p* is any positive integer, and *z* is zero, state whether the answer is *p*, *n*, or *z*.

21. (*p* ÷ *n*) + (*n* · *z*) _____

22. (*p* · *n*) · (*n* ÷ *n*) _____

ART CONNECTION

23. Industries often lose money in wasting raw materials. Find out how much a ceramics company was losing every week from tile breakage. The raw materials for 1 day cost $2,000, and 10,000 floor tiles were produced. These tiles were then packaged 50 tiles per box and stored in a warehouse. Each day 4 boxes of tiles were broken during handling. How much money was lost for a 5-day working week?

_____

Properties of Integers

Name the properties that are used.

1. $4 \cdot {}^-13 = (4 \cdot {}^-8) + (4 \cdot {}^-5) = {}^-32 + {}^-20 = {}^-52$

_____

2. $(7 + {}^-18) + 13 = ({}^-18 + 7) + 13 = {}^-18 + (7 + 13) = {}^-18 + 20 = 2$

_____

3. $3 \cdot ({}^-4 \cdot {}^-6) = (3 \cdot {}^-4) \cdot {}^-6 = ({}^-12) \cdot {}^-6 = 72$

_____

Complete.

4. $^-6 + 4 = 4 +$ _____

5. $^-16 + 16 = 16 +$ _____

6. $^-10 +$ _____ $= {}^-10$

7. _____ $\cdot {}^-15 = {}^-15$

8. _____ $\cdot 10 = {}^-10$

9. $8 \cdot {}^-5 = {}^-5 \cdot$ _____

10. $^-13 \cdot {}^-3 = {}^-3 \cdot$ _____

11. $^-23 \cdot {}^-14 = {}^-14 \cdot$ _____

12. $2 + ({}^-2 + 6) = ($ _____ $+ {}^-2) + 6$

13. $({}^-7 + {}^-6) + 3 = {}^-7 + ($ _____ $+ 3)$

14. $^-3 \cdot (4 + {}^-5) =$ _____ $+$ _____ $=$ _____

MIXED APPLICATIONS

15. Bret's uncle is 54 years old. That is three times as old as the sum of the ages of Bret and his brother. Bret is twice as old as his brother. How old is Bret?

_____

16. Angela spent $\frac{1}{3}$ of her money on a book and $\frac{2}{3}$ of it on a picture. If the book cost $11, how much money did she have to spend on the picture?

_____

NUMBER SENSE

17. The sum of two integers is $^-5$. Their product is $^-24$. What are the integers?

_____

79

Terminating Decimals

Change each fraction to a terminating decimal. You may wish to use a calculator.

1. $\frac{3}{20}$ _____

2. $\frac{49}{50}$ _____

3. $\frac{9}{4}$ _____

4. $\frac{13}{20}$ _____

5. $\frac{13}{5}$ _____

6. $\frac{42}{1,000}$ _____

7. $\frac{31}{50}$ _____

8. $\frac{6}{24}$ _____

9. $\frac{8}{25}$ _____

10. $\frac{3}{4}$ _____

11. $3\frac{3}{5}$ _____

12. $\frac{89}{100}$ _____

13. $\frac{127}{200}$ _____

14. $\frac{11}{50}$ _____

15. $\frac{7}{20}$ _____

16. $\frac{23}{10}$ _____

MIXED APPLICATIONS

17. Chiyo spends $\frac{7}{12}$ of an hour practicing the saxophone and $\frac{3}{5}$ of an hour practicing the piano. Which instrument does she practice the most?

_____

18. The Minkowsi family is on a summer vacation. By noon one day, they had traveled 132 miles. By evening, they had traveled 352 miles. What fraction of the day's travel had they completed by noon?

_____

19. The librarian at Chester's public library noted that 25% of the books children borrowed on Friday were mystery stories, 12% were adventure tales, and the rest were nonfiction books. What fraction of the books borrowed by children were nonfiction?

_____

20. Steve is drawing a floor plan of his apartment using a scale of 0.5 cm = 1 ft. If his living room measures $20\frac{3}{4}$ ft long and $16\frac{1}{2}$ ft wide, what measurements should he give the living room on the floor plan?

_____

NUMBER SENSE

Use mental math and the fact that $\frac{1}{8} = 12.5\%$ to express each fraction as a percent.

21. $\frac{1}{16}$ _____

22. $\frac{5}{16}$ _____

23. $\frac{7}{16}$ _____

Repeating Decimals

1. Use a calculator to find $\frac{1}{9}$.

$$1 \div 9 = \boxed{0.1111111}$$

$\frac{1}{9} =$ _____ $=$ _____

Use $\frac{1}{9} = 0.\overline{1}$ to find each fraction as a decimal.

2. $\frac{2}{9} =$ _____   **3.** $\frac{5}{9} =$ _____   **4.** $\frac{10}{9} =$ _____   **5.** $\frac{1}{45} =$ _____

Rewrite each repeating decimal. Use a bar to indicate repeating digits.

6. 0.263263… _____   **7.** 0.3812441244… _____

8. 3.113113… _____   **9.** 3.1298319831… _____

Use a calculator to express each fraction as a decimal. Use a bar to indicate repeating digits.

10. $\frac{5}{12}$ _____   **11.** $\frac{5}{3}$ _____   **12.** $\frac{8}{3}$ _____   **13.** $\frac{22}{9}$ _____

14. $\frac{10}{9}$ _____   **15.** $\frac{7}{12}$ _____   **16.** $\frac{4}{11}$ _____   **17.** $\frac{7}{18}$ _____

Express each fraction as a decimal. Use the values $\frac{1}{3} = 0.\overline{3}$.

18. $\frac{10}{3}$ _____   **19.** $\frac{11}{9}$ _____   **20.** $\frac{1}{90}$ _____

LOGICAL REASONING

21. Use $\frac{2}{3} = 0.6666\ldots = 0.\overline{6}$ to mentally find $\frac{2}{27}$, $\frac{4}{27}$, and $\frac{8}{27}$.

Then find a pattern and express as a decimal: $\frac{10}{27}$, $\frac{20}{27}$, and $\frac{80}{27}$.

_____

81

Exploring Rational Numbers

Predict whether each fraction can be changed to a terminating or repeating decimal. Then use a calculator to find the decimal.

1. $\frac{17}{80}$ _____

17 ÷ 80 =

2. $\frac{25}{32}$ _____

25 ÷ 32 =

3. $\frac{19}{48}$ _____

19 ÷ 48 =

Write each as a decimal.

4. $-\frac{11}{12}$ _____

5. $-\frac{50}{10}$ _____

6. $\frac{33}{9}$ _____

7. $5\frac{1}{8}$ _____

8. $\frac{11}{50}$ _____

9. $\frac{7}{9}$ _____

Predict whether the fraction can be changed to a terminating or a repeating decimal. Then write the decimal.

10. $\frac{5}{16}$ _____

_____

11. $\frac{9}{250}$ _____

_____

12. $\frac{3}{25}$ _____

_____

13. $\frac{6}{11}$ _____

_____

14. $\frac{5}{18}$ _____

_____

15. $\frac{7}{15}$ _____

_____

16. $\frac{11}{9}$ _____

_____

17. $\frac{6}{33}$ _____

_____

18. $\frac{3}{5}$ _____

_____

VISUAL THINKING

Every rational number can be
represented on a number line.
Express each number identified
by a letter as a ratio of two
integers and as a decimal.

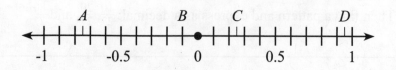

19. Point A _____

20. Point B _____

21. Point C _____

22. Point D _____

Adding Rational Numbers

1. Kendrick adds $\frac{3}{4}$ cup of chicken stock to a pot. Then he takes $\frac{3}{4}$ cup of stock out of the pot. What is the overall increase or decrease in the amount of chicken stock in the pot?

Use a positive number to represent chicken stock added to the pot and a negative number to represent chicken stock taken out of the pot.

Find $\frac{3}{4} + \left(-\frac{3}{4}\right)$. Start at _____.

Move $\left|-\frac{3}{4}\right| = \frac{3}{4}$ units to the _____.

because the second addend is _____.

The result is _____.

This means _____.

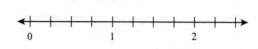

Use a number line to find each sum.

2. $3 + (-8) =$

3. $-1\frac{1}{2} + \left(-2\frac{1}{2}\right) =$

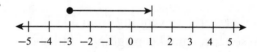

Tell what sum is modeled on each number line. Then find the sum.

4.

5.

Find each sum without using a number line.

6. $-31 + 16 =$ _____

7. $-15.3 + (-12.1) =$ _____

8. $24\frac{1}{3} + \left(-54\frac{1}{3}\right) =$ _____

9. $-40 + (-18) + 40 =$ _____

10. $15 + (-22) + 9 =$ _____

11. $-1 + 1 + (-25) =$ _____

MIXED APPLICATIONS

12. Describe a real-world situation that can be represented by the expression $-10 + (-2)$. Then find the sum and explain what it represents in terms of the situation.

_____

_____

Subtracting Rational Numbers

Use a number line to find each difference.

1. $5 - (-8) =$ _____

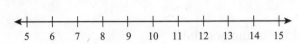

2. $-3\frac{1}{2} - 4\frac{1}{2} =$ _____

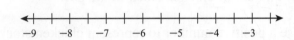

3. $-7 - 4 =$ _____

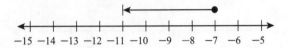

4. $-0.5 - 3.5 =$ _____

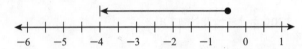

Find each difference.

5. $-14 - 22 =$ _____

6. $-12.5 - (-4.8) =$ _____

7. $\frac{1}{3} - \left(-\frac{2}{3}\right) =$ _____

8. $65 - (-14) =$ _____

9. $-\frac{2}{9} - (-3) =$ _____

10. $24\frac{3}{8} - \left(-54\frac{1}{8}\right) =$ _____

MIXED APPLICATIONS

11. A girl is snorkeling 1 meter below sea level and then dives down another 0.5 meter. How far below sea level is the girl?

_____

12. The first play of a football game resulted in a loss of 12 yards. Then a penalty resulted in another loss of 5 yards. What is the total loss or gain?

_____

13. A climber starts descending from 533 feet above sea level and keeps going until she reaches 10 feet below sea level. How many feet did she descend?

_____

14. The temperature on Sunday was -15 °C. The temperature on Monday was 12 degrees less than the temperature on Sunday. What was the temperature on Monday?

_____

15. The lowest temperature on Thursday was -20 °C. The lowest temperature on Saturday was -12 °C. What was the difference between the lowest temperatures?

_____

16. Eleni withdrew $45.00 from her savings account. She then used her debit card to buy groceries for $30.15. What was the total amount Eleni took out of her account?

_____

17. On a number line, what is the distance between -61.5 and -23.4?

_____

Multiplying Rational Numbers

Find each product.

1. -1(9) = _____

2. $\left(-\frac{2}{5}\right)\left(-\frac{12}{7}\right)$ = _____

3. (-9)(-6) = _____

4. -2(50) = _____

5. (-4)(15) = _____

6. (3)(-52.4) = _____

7. (6)$\left(-\frac{7}{15}\right)$ = _____

8. $\left(-\frac{19}{9}\right)$(0) = _____

9. (8)(-12) = _____

MIXED APPLICATIONS

10. Flora made 7 withdrawals of $75 each from her bank account. How much did she withdraw in total?

_____

11. Each of a football team's 3 plays resulted in a loss of 5 yards. How many yards in total did they lose in the 3 plays?

_____

12. The temperature dropped 2°F every hour for 6 hours. What was the total number of degrees the temperature dropped in the 6 hours?

_____

13. A mountain climber climbed down a cliff $\frac{1}{4}$ mile at a time. He did this 5 times in one day. How many miles did he climb down?

_____

14. The price of one share of Acme Company declined $3.50 per day for 4 days in a row. How much did the price of one share decline in total after the 4 days?

_____

15. In one day, 18 people each withdrew $100 from an ATM machine. How much money was withdrawn from the ATM machine?

_____

WRITER'S CORNER

16. Describe a real-world situation that can be represented by the product (-34)(3). Then find the product and explain what the product means in terms of the real-world situation.

_____

_____

Dividing Rational Numbers

Find each quotient.

1. $\dfrac{0.72}{-0.9} =$

2. $\left(\dfrac{-\frac{1}{5}}{\frac{7}{5}} \right) =$

3. $\dfrac{56}{-7} =$

4. $\dfrac{251}{4} \div \left(-\dfrac{3}{8} \right) =$

5. $\dfrac{75}{-\frac{1}{5}} =$

6. $\dfrac{-91}{-13} =$

7. $\dfrac{-\frac{3}{7}}{\frac{9}{4}} =$

8. $-\dfrac{12}{0.03} =$

9. $\dfrac{0.65}{-0.5} =$

10. $\dfrac{5}{-\frac{2}{8}} =$

11. $5\frac{1}{3} \div (-1\frac{1}{2}) =$

12. $\dfrac{-120}{-6} =$

MIXED APPLICATIONS

13. The price of one share of ABC Company declined a total of $45 in 5 days. How much did the price of one share decline, on average, per day?

_____

14. A mountain climber explored a cliff that is 225 yards high in 5 equal descents. How many yards was one descent?

_____

15. Divide 5 by 4. Is your answer a rational number? Explain.

_____

16. Should the quotient of an integer divided by a non-zero integer always be a rational number? Why or why not?

_____

EVERYDAY MATH CONNECTION

17. Describe a real-world situation that can be represented by the quotient -85 ÷ 15. Then find the quotient and explain what the quotient means in terms of the real-world situation.

_____

_____

_____

Listing All Possibilities

Make a tree diagram of all possible combinations for Exercises 1 and 2.

1. Cora is buying a new car. She can buy a two-door or a four-door car in red, blue, green, or white.

2. Blake wants to order a plate of pasta and salad. He can choose from 2 types of pasta and 3 types of salad.

MIXED APPLICATIONS

3. Rosa mixed $1\frac{1}{4}$ quarts of cranberry juice with $1\frac{3}{4}$ quarts of apple juice. How much juice did she make in all?

4. Etu picked $1\frac{1}{3}$ bushels of grapes. Rosa picked $\frac{8}{6}$ bushels of grapes. Who picked more grapes?

MIXED REVIEW

Write each fraction in simplest form.

5. $\frac{2}{12}$ _____   6. $\frac{3}{18}$ _____   7. $\frac{7}{28}$ _____   8. $\frac{10}{24}$ _____   9. $\frac{8}{16}$ _____

Find each sum or difference. Write your answer in simplest form.

10. $\begin{array}{r} \frac{1}{3} \\ +\frac{1}{2} \\ \hline \end{array}$
11. $\begin{array}{r} 4\frac{3}{8} \\ -1\frac{1}{8} \\ \hline \end{array}$
12. $\begin{array}{r} \frac{5}{9} \\ -\frac{1}{3} \\ \hline \end{array}$
13. $\begin{array}{r} 2\frac{3}{7} \\ +5\frac{1}{7} \\ \hline \end{array}$
14. $\begin{array}{r} 4\frac{5}{6} \\ -2\frac{1}{6} \\ \hline \end{array}$
15. $\begin{array}{r} 1\frac{3}{8} \\ +1\frac{3}{8} \\ \hline \end{array}$

Counting Principle

Make a tree diagram to find the number of choices in Exercises 1–3.

1.

Floor Coverings	Color
Carpet	Green
	Blue
	Rose

2.

Sweaters	Skirts
White	Plaid
Black	Striped
	Plain

3.

Paint	Trim
Brown	Tan
White	Black
Red	

Write the number of choices.

4. 2 meats, 3 vegetables _____

5. 3 coats, 4 hats _____

6. 4 cards, 8 envelopes _____

7. 5 books, 7 covers _____

MIXED APPLICATIONS

8. Fernando bought a new watch set that includes 5 watch faces and 7 colored bands. From how many different watches can he choose?

9. Each of 4 television stations offers 5 types of shows each day. From how many shows can you choose?

LANGUAGE ARTS CONNECTION

10. Taylor's English homework involves pairing 4 verbs with 4 nouns. How many different sentences can he make?

Exploring Combinations

Use this information for Exercises 1–5.

David ordered a subway sandwich. His choice of ingredients was: ham, turkey, roast beef, salami, lettuce, and pickles. Follow the steps below to find out how many different ways David could order a sandwich with 2 ingredients.

Mark 6 cards with the letters H, T, R, S, L, and P to represent the ingredients.

1. List all the different ways you can choose the second ingredient when H is the first ingredient. Use the form (H, T).

   _____

2. Repeat this process using each of the other choices for the first ingredient.

   _____

   _____

3. Since a sandwich with ham and turkey is the same as a sandwich with turkey and ham, cross out the pairs that reverse the pairs already listed. How many pairs remain in the list?

   _____

4. Use your cross-out pattern to find an addition sentence to show the number of combinations of 6 ingredients taken 2 at a time.

   _____

5. How many different 2-letter combinations can you make from the first 8 letters of the alphabet? Remember: (A, B) is the same as (B, A).

   _____

VISUAL THINKING

6. Mark 5 points around a circle. How many triangles can be drawn by connecting the points so that all the vertices of the triangles lie on the circle?

   _____

Exploring Permutations

Use this information to solve Exercises 1–6.

John, Mary, Andrew, Chantelle, and Scott are seated in a row of 5 seats. Follow the steps below to find out in how many different ways they can be seated.

Mark 5 cards J, M, A, C, and S to represent the 5 people.

1. How many choices of seats does the first person have? _____

2. How many seats are left for the second person? _____

3. How many seats are then left for the third person? _____

4. How many seats are then left for the fourth person? _____

5. How many seats remain for the fifth person? _____

6. Find the number of different arrangements of the 5 people. Could you do this by multiplying $5 \times 4 \times 3 \times 2 \times 1$? Explain.

_____

_____

7. In how many ways can 7 students be seated at 7 desks?

_____

8. In how many different ways can 6 people line up in a lunch line?

_____

9. There are 8 candidates running for the offices of president, vice-president, secretary, treasurer, and representative. How many different results could there be in the election? Remember, Person 1 being elected president is different from Person 1 being elected to another office.

_____

NUMBER SENSE

The product of $4 \times 3 \times 2 \times 1$ is a special product called "4 factorial."
It is symbolized by the expression 4! The value of 4! is 24.

Find the value of these factorial expressions.

10. 5! _____   11. 6! _____   12. 7! _____   13. 9! _____

Problem-Solving Strategy

MAKE AN ORGANIZED LIST

Julia and Samuel are studying to be engineers. Five of their required courses are Algebra, Calculus, Physics, Chemistry, and Computer Programming. The courses are assigned randomly by a computer.

Organize a list of all possible ways they could be assigned the courses if they each take one course. Then find each probability.

1. Julia and Samuel will be taking the same course.

_____

2. They will be taking different courses.

_____

3. Neither one will be in Chemistry or Computer Programming.

_____

4. Julia will be in either Algebra or Physics, and Samuel will be in either Calculus or Chemistry.

_____

MIXED APPLICATIONS

5. Clarisa left a 15% tip of $1.80 for a haircut. How much was the cost of the haircut without the tip?

_____

6. Out of 8 candidates (A, B, C, D, E, F, G, H), 2 will be chosen Chairperson and Secretary of a committee. In how many ways can the two offices be filled?

_____

WRITER'S CORNER

7. There are five movies being shown at the Value Theater. Write a problem about the probability of two or three people attending the same movie at the same time. Solve.

_____

_____

_____

Fundamental Counting Principle

Find the total number of choices.

1. ties: red, blue, green

   shirts: white, pink

   _____

2. drink: apple juice

   sandwich: hamburger, grilled cheese

   _____

3. picnics: national park, zoo

   dates: March, April

   _____

4. pattern: stripes, round, plain

   size: small, medium, large

   _____

Mr. Ames is going to buy a new TV. The table shows his choices. Use the table for Exercises 5–7.

5. How many choices does Mr. Ames have in all?

   _____

Types	Sizes	Options
Plasma	13 in.	HDMI
LED	20 in.	Wireless
	24 in.	Picture in Picture

6. If Mr. Ames does not want any options, how many choices does he have?

   _____

7. If Mr. Ames wants a 20-in. plasma TV, how many options does he have?

   _____

MIXED APPLICATIONS

8. A restaurant has 5 appetizers, 10 entrees, and 6 salads. In how many different ways can a person order a meal that includes an appetizer, an entrée, and a salad?

   _____

9. If 20 eggs cost $2.00, what is the cost of a dozen eggs?

   _____

WRITER'S CORNER

10. Write a problem involving choices and shopping. Exchange problems with a friend. Solve.

   _____

   _____

Introduction to Chance Events

Use this information for Exercises 1–6.

Marcia draws one coin from a container to help her decide where she will go to dinner. In the container are 4 pennies, 4 nickels, 2 dimes, and 3 quarters.

Coins	Outcomes
Penny	Dinner at a fast-food restaurant
Nickel	Dinner at a family restaurant
Dime	Dinner at a fancy restaurant
Quarter	Dinner at home

Are the outcomes in each pair likely?

1. Dinner at a fast-food restaurant. Dinner at a family restaurant.

_____

2. Dinner at home. Dinner at a fancy restaurant.

_____

3. Dinner at a fast-food restaurant. Dinner at home.

_____

4. Dinner at a fancy restaurant. Dinner at a family restaurant.

_____

Write whether each event is *certain*, *impossible*, or *neither*.

5. Marcia goes out to dinner.

_____

6. Marcia eats dinner.

_____

MIXED APPLICATIONS

7. In Marcia's coin container, what is the ratio of quarters to nickels?

_____

8. What percent of Marcia's coins are worth 10¢ or more?

_____

9. A jar has 6 marbles, 4 red and 2 blue. What is the ratio of blue to red marbles?

_____

LOGICAL REASONING

10. The sum of each pair of numbers on opposite sides of a number cube (with dots 1 to 6) equals 7. Find the numbers that could be on each pair of opposite sides.

_____

Probability of a Simple Event

Use the spinner and table for Exercises 1–9

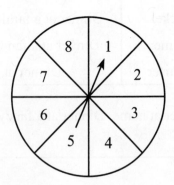

Item	Number
penny	1
nickel	2
dime	3
quarter	4
2 dimes	5
2 quarters	6
dollar	7
5 nickels	8

Write the probability of each event as a fraction in simplest form.

1. a penny _____

2. 1 quarter _____

3. at least 25¢ _____

4. at least 50¢ _____

5. at most 25¢ _____

6. at most 50¢ _____

7. even _____

8. composite number _____

9. a 7 _____

MIXED APPLICATIONS

10. There are 10 sweaters in a drawer. Four of them are blue; 2 are green. In simplest form, write the probability of choosing a blue sweater.

_____

11. In Exercise 10, what is the probability of choosing a green sweater?

_____

WRITER'S CORNER

12. Choose five possible breakfast foods. Draw a spinner so that your favorite breakfast food has the greatest probability of being selected. Write a problem about the probability of selecting each breakfast item.

_____

_____

_____

Exploring Experimental Probability

Use the spinner for Exercises 1–6.

You spin this spinner 10 times and land
on blue 3 times.

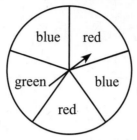

1. What is the experimental probability of
   landing on blue?

   _____

2. List the possible outcomes for the spinner.

   _____

3. What is the mathematical probability of
   landing on blue?

   _____

4. Is the experimental probability of $\frac{3}{10}$ close
   to the mathematical probability of landing on
   blue? Explain.

   _____

5. If you spin this spinner 50 times, would
   it be reasonable to land on blue 22 times?
   Explain.

   _____

6. You spin the spinner 500 times. Use
   mathematical probability to predict the
   number of times you will land on red.

   _____

7. You roll a number cube 30 times. Predict how
   many times it will show a 1.

   _____

8. You will roll a number cube 50 times.
   Predict how many times it will land on
   an even number.

   _____

9. You spin the spinner at the top of this page
   20 times. Predict the number of times it will
   not land on red.

   _____

10. You toss a coin 40 times. Predict how many
    times it will land on tails.

    _____

EVERYDAY MATH CONNECTION

11. Shane is on a baseball team. He averages 6 hits in 30 times at bat.
    How many hits would you expect him to have after 180 times at bat?

    _____

Probability with Spinners

Use the spinner for Exercises 1–4.

1. How many sections does the spinner have? How many colors?

   _____

2. What are the possible outcomes of spinning the spinner?

   _____

3. What is the probability of the spinner landing on yellow? on green? on white?

   _____

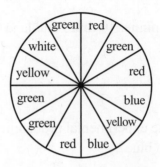

4. What is the probability of the spinner landing on green or yellow or blue?

   _____

Use the spinner for Exercises 5–10.

5. What are the possible outcomes of spinning the spinner?

   _____

6. What is the probability of the spinner landing on a name with 3 letters in it? 4 letters in it? 5 letters in it?

   _____

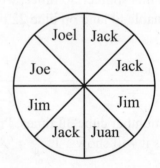

Suppose you spin the spinner 8 times. How many times do you think it will land on each name?

7. Joel _____   8. Jack _____   9. Joe _____   10. Jim _____

┌─────────────────────┐
│ **VISUAL THINKING** │
└─────────────────────┘

11. Draw a spinner. Make up some questions about your spinner.

   _____

   _____

Name _____ Date _____

Probability with Marbles

Use this information for Exercises 1 and 2.

A bag of marbles has 10 white marbles, 5 blue marbles, 40 red marbles, and 25 yellow marbles.

1. What are the possible outcomes for picking a marble without looking?

   _____

2. What color marble is most likely to be picked?

   _____

Use this information for Exercises 3–8.

Suppose you pick one marble from the bag. Write a fraction for the probability that the marble will be each color.

3. blue

   _____

4. red

   _____

5. yellow

   _____

6. white

   _____

7. blue or yellow

   _____

8. white, blue, red, or yellow

   _____

MIXED APPLICATIONS

9. To decide what day each member of the family does the dishes, each person draws the name of a day of the week from a hat. What is the probability of drawing a day that begins with T?

   _____

10. Andy has 4 brothers and 2 sisters. What is the ratio of boys to girls in his family?

    _____

MIXED REVIEW

Find the perimeter and area of each figure.

11.

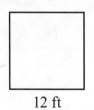

12 ft

Perimeter _____

Area _____

12.

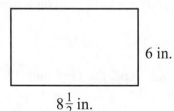

6 in.

$8\frac{1}{2}$ in.

Perimeter _____

Area _____

13.

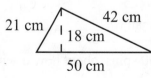

21 cm   42 cm

18 cm

50 cm

Perimeter _____

Area _____

Theoretical Probability

Use this information and the chart to complete Exercises 1 and 2.

At a school fair, you have a choice of randomly picking a ball from Basket A or Basket B. Basket A has 5 green balls, 3 red balls, and 8 yellow balls. Basket B has 7 green balls, 4 red balls, and 9 yellow balls. You can win a digital book reader if you pick a red ball.

	Basket A	Basket B
Total Number of Outcomes		
Number of Red Balls		
$P(\text{win}) = $ $\dfrac{\text{Number of red balls}}{\text{Total number of outcomes}}$		

1. Complete the chart. Write each answer in simplest form.

2. Which basket should you choose if you want the better chance of winning? _____

3. Jim has 4 nickels, 6 pennies, 4 dimes, and 2 quarters in his pocket. He picks a coin at random. What is the probability that he will pick a nickel or a dime? Write your answer as a fraction, as a decimal, and as a percent.

_____

Use this information to complete Exercises 4–6.

A class has 12 boys and 15 girls. The teacher randomly picks one child to lead the class in singing.

4. What is the probability that the teacher picks a boy? _____

5. What is the probability that the teacher picks a girl? _____

6. Describe two different ways you could find the answer to Exercise 5.

_____

Use the spinner for Exercises 7–10.

7. In 20 spins, about how often can you expect to land on a number evenly divisible by 2? _____

8. In 150 spins, about how often can you expect to land on a number less than 6? _____

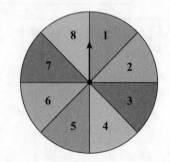

9. In 200 spins, about how often can you expect to land on a 1? _____

10. Rudolfo says there is a greater chance of landing on an even number than on an odd number. What is his error?

_____

Experimental Probability

Use the table to complete Exercises 1 and 2.

1. Toss a coin at least 20 times. Record the outcomes in the table.

2. What do you think would happen if you performed more trials?

   _____

   _____

Tossing of Coin	Number of Times	Experimental Probability
Heads		
Tails		

3. Sonja has a bag of ping pong balls. She removed one ball, recorded the marking, and then placed it back in the bag. She repeated this process several times and recorded her results in the table. Find the experimental probability of each marked ping pong ball. Write your answers in simplest form.

Type	Frequency
Stripes	12
Polka dots	13
Stars	18
Solid color	17
Squares	10

   Stripes: _____ Polka dots: _____

   Stars: _____ Solid color: _____ Squares: _____

Use a spinner with six equal sections for Exercises 4–6.

4. What is the theoretical probability of landing on a specific section of your spinner?

   _____

5. Spin the spinner 30 times. Complete the table.

Color or Numbered Section						
Frequency						
Experimental Probability						

6. Look at the tables you completed. How do the experimental probabilities compare with the theoretical probabilities?

   _____

CRITICAL THINKING

7. Patricia finds that the experimental probability of her dog wanting to go outside between 4 P.M. and 5 P.M. is $\frac{7}{12}$. About what percent of the time does her dog not want to go out between 4 P.M. and 5 P.M.?

   _____

Compound Events

Use the table to complete Exercises 1–3.

Drake rolls two number cubes each containing the numbers from 1 to 6 on the 6 faces of the cube.

1. Complete the table to find the sample space for rolling a particular product on two number cubes.

	1	2	3	4	5	6
1						
2						
3						
4						
5						
6						

2. What is the probability that the product of the two numbers Drake rolls is a multiple of 4?

_____

3. What is the probability that the product of the two numbers Drake rolls is less than 13?

_____

Use this information to complete Exercises 4 and 5.

Mattias gets dressed in the dark one morning and chooses his clothes at random. He chooses a shirt (green, red, or yellow), a pair of pants (black or blue), and a pair of sneakers (checkered or red).

4. Use the space at right to make a tree diagram to find the sample space.

5. What is the probability that Mattias picks an outfit at random that includes red sneakers?

_____

Use this information to complete Exercises 6 and 7.

Lockers at Erin's gym have a lock with a randomly assigned three-digit code. The code uses the digits 2, 3, or 8. Any of these numbers may be repeated.

6. Use the space at right to make an organized list to find the sample space.

7. What is the probability that Erin's locker has a code with at least one 8?

_____

Independent Events and Sample Space

Use this information to complete Exercises 1 and 2.

Candy is deciding whether to buy a car, a truck, or a van.
She can choose a 4-speed, 5-speed, or automatic transmission.

1. Make a diagram to show all of Candy's possible choices.

2. What is the probability that Candy will choose to buy a 5-speed truck? _____

MIXED APPLICATIONS

3. Hisako bought 1 of 400 raffle tickets and 1 of 10 tickets to win a cake at the school fair. Does Hisako have a better chance to win the raffle prize or the cake?

_____

4. Linda bought 4 blouses and 4 skirts. How many skirt-and-blouse outfits can she make?

_____

MIXED REVIEW

Evaluate each algebraic expression.

5. $\frac{n}{10}$, for $n = 100$ _____

6. $5.6c$, for $c = 1.2$ _____

Tell which operation you use to solve each equation. Then solve.

7. $45z = 450$ _____

8. $\frac{m}{13} = 42$ _____

Draw a picture to show the number of choices.

9. 2 CDs, 4 cases

10. 3 belts, 3 slacks

Independent Events

Spin this spinner and roll a cube number 1–6 at the same time. Find each probability.

1. red and a 6 _____

2. green and a 2 _____

3. blue and not 3 _____

4. yellow and an
   even number _____

5. purple and a 4 _____

6. blue and a 7 _____

Roll a number cube two times. Find each probability.

7. a 1 and then a 5 _____

8. a 2 and then an odd number _____

9. an even number and then a 1 _____

10. an even number
    and then an odd number _____

MIXED APPLICATIONS

Use this information to find each probability.

A box contains 4 blue marbles, 5 red marbles, 2 green marbles, and 1 purple marble.
You pick a marble at random, replace it, and then pick another marble at random.

11. blue and then red _____

12. green and then purple _____

13. blue, blue, and then red _____

14. blue and then blue _____

MIXED REVIEW

Write a fraction for each percent. Solve.

15. 75% of 96

16. 42% of 100

17. 9% of 40

_____

_____

_____

Write a decimal for each percent. Solve.

18. 5% of 36

19. 12% of 500

20. $3\frac{1}{2}$ % of 500

_____

_____

_____

Independent Events and Sample Space

Find each probability.

Two nickels are tossed and a number cube is rolled.

1. p(two heads, 4)

_____

2. p(one tail, odd number)

_____

3. p(two tails, even number)

_____

4. p(two heads, not 3)

_____

5. p(not tails, 7)

_____

6. p(one tail, 2 or 4)

_____

Find each probability.

You spin the spinners.

7. p(blue, 2)

_____

8. p(red, 6)

_____

9. p(not blue, odd number)

_____

10. p(red, not 8)

_____

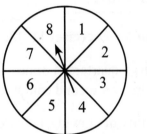 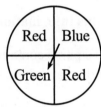

11. p(red, 5, red)

_____

12. p(not red, 8)

_____

MIXED APPLICATIONS

13. Sheila throws two coins at a time. She will win the game if she gets two like events. What is the probability she will win?

_____

14. Joe correctly answered 70% of the questions on a test. There were 50 questions. How many questions did Joe answer correctly?

_____

MIXED REVIEW

Find each product.

15. $\frac{1}{2} \times \frac{1}{4}$ _____

16. $\frac{2}{3} \times \frac{1}{5}$ _____

17. $\frac{34}{4} \times \frac{1}{3}$ _____

18. Find the mean, median, and mode of 73, 64, 92, 73, 83, 79, 96.

_____

103

Dependent Events

Find each probability.

A box contains 4 white crayons, 3 red crayons, 3 blue crayons, and 2 purple crayons.
You pick a crayon at random and then draw a second crayon without replacing the first.

1. p(white, then red) _____

2. p(red, then blue) _____

3. p(purple, then white) _____

4. p(white, then white) _____

5. p(red, then red) _____

6. p(blue, then blue) _____

7. p(purple, then purple) _____

8. p(red, then white) _____

9. p(purple, then black) _____

10. p(blue, then red) _____

MIXED APPLICATIONS

Use this information for Exercises 11–13.

Mimi's purse contains 5 quarters, 4 dimes, 4 nickels, and 2 pennies. Mimi draws one coin
at random and then draws a second coin without replacing the first.

11. Find the probability of drawing a quarter and
then a dime.

12. Find the probability of drawing a quarter and
then another quarter.

13. Write a ratio for the chance of drawing
a dime on the first draw and a nickel on
the second draw.

14. Sean has 10 black socks, 6 blue socks, and
2 brown socks in his drawer. He selects
1 sock and then another without replacing
the first. What is the probability that he will
select 2 black socks?

NUMBER SENSE

15. How many different ratios can be made with the digits 1, 2, 4, 6, and 8? Write
each ratio in fraction form. If the two ratios are equivalent, they are not different.

Probability of Dependent Events

Find each probability.

A jar contains 2 green, 3 white, and 5 black balls. The balls are selected at random, one at a time, and not replaced.

1. p(white, then green) _____

2. p(green, then black) _____

3. p(black, then black) _____

4. p(black, then black, then black) _____

5. p(white, then white, then green) _____

6. p(white, then green, then green) _____

7. p(black, then green, then white) _____

Find each probability.

A box contains 5 red marbles, 3 blue marbles, and 7 white marbles. The marbles are selected at random, one at a time, and not replaced.

8. p(red, then blue) _____

9. p(red, then white) _____

10. p(red, then white, then blue) _____

11. p(white, then white, then white) _____

MIXED APPLICATIONS

12. Janette picks from a deck of 52 playing cards. What is the probability that she will pick a king?

_____

13. In Exercise 12, if Janette picks up a second card without replacing the first one, what is the probability that she will pick a king again?

_____

WRITER'S CORNER

14. Throw a number cube 25 times. Write the outcome of each throw. Write a

probability question based on your outcomes. Solve. _____

Name _____ Date _____

Understanding Simulations

1. A computer program generates 52 random names starting with the letters *A*, *B*, *C*, or *D*. How many names would you expect to start with *B*?

   _____

2. A computer program generates the digits *1, 2, 3* at random 50 times. Write a problem that this program could simulate.

   _____

MIXED APPLICATIONS

3. There are 10 boys and 10 girls in a class. There are two computers to be used by one boy and one girl. How many possible combinations of students can use the computers?

   _____

4. Mrs. Larson bought twice as many bananas as apples. If she bought 2 oranges and the number of oranges was $\frac{1}{3}$ the number of apples, how many bananas did she buy?

   _____

5. On a certain jet, the ratio of first-class to economy-class passengers is 1:4. If there are 60 first-class passengers, how many passengers are there in all?

   _____

6. Mrs. Brady is considering a trip to Hawaii, Florida, or Alaska. She has eight children, and $\frac{1}{4}$ pick Florida. Three of them pick Alaska. The rest pick Hawaii. How many children pick Hawaii?

   _____

WRITER'S CORNER

7. A computer program generates the digits 1 to 5 at random 50 times. Write a problem that this program could simulate.

   _____

   _____

Name _____ Date _____

Exploring Simulations

Use a large jar full of dried beans. Grab a handful of beans, count them, and mark a colored "x" on each bean. Put the marked beans back in the jar and mix all the beans together. Now grab another handful of beans.

1. Write a fraction to show the ratio of those marked "x" to the total number of beans in your new handful, or sample.

   _____

2. Now write a proportion to estimate the number of beans in the jar.

   $$\frac{\text{Marked ("}x\text{") in new sample}}{\text{Total in new sample}} = \frac{\text{total marked}}{\text{total in jar}}$$

      $x = $ _____

3. Let the handful of beans from the first handful represent the first sample of birds

   an ecology worker catches and marks. What does the x represent? _____

4. How would you use a table of 20 random digits containing digits 0 through 9 to simulate 100 spins of a 10-item spinner?

   _____

   _____

   _____

MIXED REVIEW

5. What percent of 25 is 10? _____

6. 25% of what number is 6? _____

7. What number is 15% of 40? _____

8. What percent of 36 is 18? _____

9. 384 is 32% of what number? _____

10. What number is $37\frac{1}{2}$% of 112? _____

Working with Simulations

Use this information to complete Exercises 1–4.

At a company that makes soda cans, something went wrong with the machine that stamps the type of soda on the can. For about 3 hours, it stamped *orange juice* on cans of grapefruit juice, it stamped *grapefruit juice* on cans of cola, and it did not stamp some of the cans at all. The machine stamps about 1,500 cans per hour.

1. The plant foreman decided to run the machine for $\frac{1}{2}$ hr. What information can be gained from this trial run?

   _____

   _____

   _____

2. The plant foreman found that out of 750 cans stamped in the $\frac{1}{2}$-hour run, 150 were not stamped. About how many were not stamped in 3 hours?

   _____

3. Of the 750 cans in the trial run, 500 were incorrectly stamped *orange juice*. About how many cans were incorrectly stamped *orange juice* in 3 hours?

   _____

4. Use the information from Exercises 2 and 3. Suppose the remainder of the 750 cans were incorrectly stamped grapefruit juice. About how many cans were incorrectly stamped *grapefruit juice* in 3 hours?

   _____

MIXED APPLICATIONS

5. The label on a box is either right side up (R) or upside down (U). In how many different ways can the labels on a group of 8 boxes appear?

   _____

6. Use the information from Exercises 1-4. About how many cans were incorrectly stamped *orange juice* or *grapefruit juice* in 2 hours?

   _____

LOGICAL REASONING

7. You spin 4 spinners independently. The probabilities of each spinner landing on 3 are $\frac{1}{8}$, $\frac{3}{6}$, $\frac{1}{4}$, and $\frac{3}{8}$, respectively. Find the probability of p(3, 3, 3, 3).

   _____

   _____

Conducting a Simulation

Use the information in the tables to answer Exercises 1–4.

1. Anthony is developing a probability simulation and has created this table. He determines that the number 1 will measure his outcome. What is the experimental probability of getting at least one 1 in a trial?

   _____

   _____

2. Elisa is developing a probability simulation and has created a table showing 10 trials. She determines that the 2 will measure her outcome. What is the experimental probability of getting at least one 2 in a trial?

   _____

   _____

3. Luis is developing a probability simulation and has created a table showing 10 trials. He determines that the 0 will measure his outcome. What is the experimental probability of getting at least one 0 in a trial?

   _____

   _____

4. Ari is developing a probability simulation and has created the table below. He determines that the number 3 will measure his outcome. What is the experimental probability of getting at least one 3 in a trial?

   _____

   _____

Trial	Random Numbers	Outcome
1	1 3 1 5 6	2
2	9 1 1 3 0	2
3	3 0 6 5 1	1
4	1 2 0 8 8	1
5	9 4 3 3 4	0
6	2 1 0 3 8	1
7	4 0 9 2 8	0
8	0 7 8 1 6	1
9	0 7 1 5 2	1
10	8 2 5 8 5	0

Trial	Random Numbers	Outcomes
1	2 5 9 9 1	1
2	3 2 7 0 4	1
3	8 2 1 9 5	1
4	6 6 6 7 4	0
5	4 3 4 0 3	0
6	2 6 6 7 5	1
7	0 3 1 8 5	0
8	5 9 5 6 8	0
9	0 4 7 5 2	1
10	1 1 7 3 6	0

Trial	Random Numbers	Outcome
1	4 9 1 0 4	1
2	3 7 2 6 5	0
3	4 6 0 2 7	1
4	4 6 1 0 5	1
5	6 2 6 7 8	0
6	6 2 4 4 4	0
7	5 9 1 2 8	0
8	0 0 3 4 4	2
9	3 8 1 9 6	0
10	3 3 7 3 3	0

Trial	Random Numbers	Outcomes
1	6 1 1 6 7	0
2	4 5 1 4 5	0
3	4 4 4 8 2	0
4	6 1 1 0 4	0
5	4 2 3 4 6	1
6	4 3 4 1 3	2
7	9 1 4 8 0	0
8	1 1 3 7 0	1
9	3 6 7 3 0	0
10	8 3 5 9 8	1

109

Name _____ Date _____

Circles

Use Figure A for Exercises 1–7. Find and name the circle and its parts.

1. center _____

2. two diameters _____

3. two radii _____

4. two chords _____

5. circle _____

6. intersecting line segments _____

7. If $UV = 5$ cm, what is VY? WU? _____

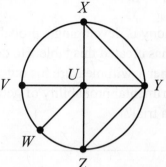

Figure A

Use Figure B for Exercises 8–12.

8. What is $\overline{AE}$? _____

9. What is $\overline{BD}$? _____

10. What is $\overline{AC}$? _____

11. What is $\overline{CD}$? _____

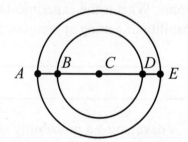

Figure B

MIXED APPLICATIONS

12. A circular pond has a diameter of 100 ft. A fountain is placed in the center of the pond. How far from the edge of the pond is the center of the fountain?

_____

13. A circular patio with a diameter of 12 ft is made of bricks. Each brick is 6 in. long. A row of bricks is laid end-to-end along the diameter of the circle. How many bricks are laid along the diameter?

_____

MIXED REVIEW

Write each percent as a decimal.

14. 45% _____   15. 36% _____   16. 5% _____   17. 40% _____

Write each percent as a fraction in simplest form.

18. 40% _____   19. 75% _____   20. 65% _____   21. 36% _____

Exploring Circumference of a Circle

Find the circumference. Use $\frac{22}{7}$ for π.

1. diameter = 14 in. _____

2. diameter = 42 in. _____

3. diameter = 28 in. _____

4. radius = 14 in. _____

5 radius = 7 cm _____

6. radius = 21 ft _____

Find each circumference. Use 3.14 for π. Round your answer to the nearest tenth. You may want to use a calculator.

7.

_____

8.

_____

9.

_____

10.

_____

11.

_____

12.

_____

13. diameter = 4 cm _____

14. diameter = 9 in. _____

15. radius = 15 m _____

16. radius is 9 cm _____

17. radius is 18 ft _____

18. radius is 20 mm _____

CALCULATOR

19. How could you find the circumference of many different circles with a calculator without punching in 3.14 for every problem?

_____

_____

Name _____ Date _____

Circumference of Circles

Find each circumference. Use 3.14 for π.

1.
2 cm

_____

2.
7 in.

_____

3.
12 m

_____

4.
15 ft

_____

Find each circumference to the nearest whole number.

5. $d = 9$ m _____

6. $d = 2.1$ cm _____

7. $r = 6.1$ cm _____

8. $r = 7.3$ mm _____

9. $d = 56$ m _____

10. $d = 63$ m _____

11. $r = 2.8$ cm _____

12. $r = 4\frac{1}{5}$ cm _____

Find each circumference to the nearest tenth. Use 3.14 for π.

13. $d = 6.4$ mm _____

14. $r = 0.8$ cm _____

15. $r = 5.6$ cm _____

16. $d = 21.1$ cm _____

MIXED APPLICATIONS

17. A tabletop is shaped like a square with half-circles on two ends. One side of the square is 0.8 m. To the nearest meter, what is the perimeter of the tabletop?

0.8 m

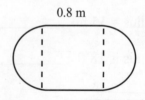

_____

18. A sundial in a park has a circumference of 57 ft. Find the radius to the nearest foot.

_____

NUMBER SENSE

19. When a number is divided by –3, the result is 12 more than the number. What is the number?

_____

112

Finding Circumference

Find the circumference to the nearest hundredth. Use 3.14 for π.

1. *r* = 4.055 cm _____

2. *r* = 0.03 cm _____

3. *d* = 0.48 m _____

4. *d* = 0.92 km _____

Find the circumference. Use $\frac{22}{7}$ for π.

5. *r* = 7 in. _____

6. *r* = 21 yd _____

7. *d* = 56 ft _____

8. *r* = 35 ft _____

Find the diameter of each circle. The circumference is given. Use 3.14 for π.

9. 131.88 ft _____   10. 1.57 m _____   11. 314 in. _____

12. Which is greater, the perimeter of the square or

the circumference of the circle? _____

12 m

MIXED APPLICATIONS

13. A tree is surrounded with a circular retaining wall 3 m in diameter. What is the circumference of the retaining wall?

_____

14. A circular fountain will be surrounded by a fence. If the radius of the fountain is 5 ft, what is the amount of fencing needed?

_____

MIXED REVIEW

Find the perimeter of the following squares. The length of a side is given.

15. 5 cm _____   16. 20 m _____   17. 4 km _____

18. 6 cm _____   19. 7 yd _____

Find each product.

20. -7 × -3 = _____

21. 18 × -3 = _____

22. 2 × -14 · -2 = _____

113

Problem-Solving Strategy

USE A FORMULA

Use a formula to solve.

1. A swimming pool is in the shape of a circle. The circumference is 6.594 m. What is the diameter?

_____

2. The circumference of a bike tire is 69.08 in. What is the diameter?

_____

3. The diameter of a can of corn is 77 mm. What is the circumference?

_____

4. The diameter of a basketball is 245 cm. What is the circumference?

_____

MIXED APPLICATIONS

5. Scott makes monthly deposits to his savings account. During the past four months, he made the following deposits: $25, $30, $40, $60. If the pattern continues, how much will Scott deposit in the sixth month?

_____

6. Julia deposited $\frac{1}{2}$ her paycheck in her savings account and $\frac{1}{4}$ of it in her checking account. She spent $22.76 of it on a T-shirt and then spent $\frac{1}{4}$ of what was left of her paycheck on lunch. When she arrived home, she had $16.68 of her paycheck left. How much money did Julia receive in her paycheck?

_____

7. Rita completed a 50-mile bike race in $2\frac{1}{4}$ hours. What was her average speed?

_____

8. The circumference of a highlight marker is about 21.98 mm. Find the diameter of the marker.

_____

SCIENCE CONNECTION

9. In a science experiment, the number of flowers doubles from one day to the next. If on day 1 there are 5 flowers, how many flowers are there on day 3?

_____

Area of Circles

Find the area of each circle. Use 3.14 for π. Round to the nearest tenth.

1. $r = 10$ in. _____ **2.** $d = 8$ in. _____ **3.** $r = 5$ m _____

4. $d = 6$ ft _____ **5.** $r = 1.5$ in. _____ **6.** $d = 6.4$ cm _____

7. $r = 0.9$ m _____ **8.** $r = 14.4$ in. _____ **9.** $d = 7$ cm _____

10. $d = 9$ ft _____ **11.** $d = 15$ m _____ **12.** $d = 45$ in. _____

MIXED APPLICATIONS

13. Jerry has a picture in the shape of a circle. The diameter is 46 cm. What is the circumference of the picture?

_____

14. A furniture store delivers without charge to any location within 100 mi of the store. About what is the area of this region?

_____

15. Inés set 6 drinking glasses with circular bottoms next to each other in a row on a table. If each glass has a circumference of about 9.4 in., about what is the length of the row of glasses?

_____

16. A farm has a circular pond with a small circular island in the center. The diameter of the pond is 50 ft. The diameter of the island is 10 ft. What is the area of the pond that is water?

_____

LOGICAL REASONING

17. A cow is tied on a 50-foot rope to the corner of a 20-ft by 50-ft rectangular building. The cow can graze on any of the grass it can reach. What is the area on which the cow can graze? Draw a diagram to support your answer.

_____

_____

115

More Area of Circles

Find the area of each circle to the nearest whole number. Use 3.14 for π.

1.
10 cm

_____

2.
2.6 cm

_____

3.
4.5 m

_____

4.
20.6 cm

_____

5.
1.5 m

_____

6.
8.2 cm

_____

7.
14.5 m

_____

8.
24.6 m

_____

Find the area of each circle to the nearest tenth.

9. $r = 2$ m _____   10. $r = 9$ m _____   11. $d = 12$ m _____

Find the area of each circle to the nearest hundredth.

12. $r = 0.8$ in. _____   13. $d = 1.4$ ft _____   14. $d = 0.72$ m _____

MIXED APPLICATIONS

Use this information for Exercises 15–17.

Anzu made a dartboard like the one shown. The circle in the middle is the bulls-eye.

15. What is the area of the bulls-eye? _____

16. What is the area of the outer rim? _____

17. The outer rim is how many times

as large as the bulls-eye? _____

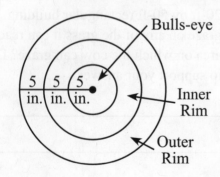

NUMBER SENSE

18. Fill in the boxes using 3, 4, 5, and 7

$$2^{\square} + \square^2 = \square^{\square}$$

Areas of Circles and Inscribed Figures

Find each area to the nearest hundredth. Use 3.14 for π.

1.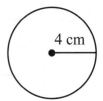

2.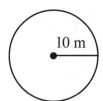

3.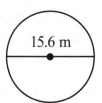

_____   _____   _____

Find the area of each shaded region.

4.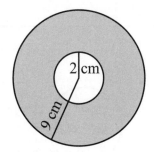

5.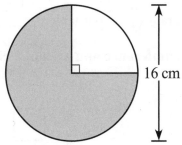

6.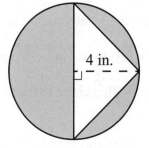

_____   _____   _____

MIXED APPLICATIONS

7. A satellite antenna is circular in shape. If the diameter is 10 m, what is the area of the antenna?

_____

8. A certain clock has a circular face. If the area of the face is 113.04 in.², what is the circumference?

_____

MIXED REVIEW

Evaluate each expression for $n = 10$.

9. $8n$ _____   10. $n + 12$ _____   11. $\frac{n}{2}$ _____   12. $2n + 1$ _____

Write a decimal for each fraction.

13. $\frac{3}{2}$ _____   14. $\frac{4}{25}$ _____   15. $\frac{3}{50}$ _____   16. $\frac{14}{28}$ _____

Unit 12
Core Skills Math, Grade 7

Circumference and Area of Circles

1. Use a measuring tape to find the circumference of five circular objects. Then measure the distance across each item to find its diameter. Record the measurements of each object in the table.

2. Divide the circumference of each object by its diameter. Round your answer to the nearest hundredth.

Object	Circumference C	Diameter d	$\frac{C}{d}$

_____

3. Describe what you notice about the ratio $\frac{C}{d}$ in your table. _____

Find the relationship between the circumference and area of a circle.

4. Start with a circle that has radius r.

   Solve the equation $C = 2\pi r$ for r. $r = \dfrac{\Box}{\Box}$

   Substitute your expression for r in the formula for area of a circle. $A = \pi \left(\dfrac{\Box}{\Box} \right)^2$

   Square the term in the parentheses. $A = \pi \left(\dfrac{\Box^2}{\Box^2 \cdot \Box^2} \right)$

   Evaluate the power. $A = \dfrac{\Box \cdot \Box}{\Box \cdot \Box^2}$

   Simplify. $A = \dfrac{\Box^2}{\Box \cdot \Box}$

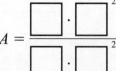

   Solve for C^2. $C^2 = 4\,\Box\,\Box$

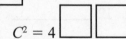

   The circumference of the circle squared is equal to _____.

Find the area of each circle given the circumference. Give your answers in terms of π.

5. $C = 8\pi$; $A = $ _____

6. $C = \pi$; $A = $ _____

7. $C = 2\pi$; $A = $ _____

Area: Parallelograms and Triangles

Find the area of each figure.

1.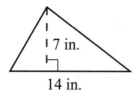

18 cm · 6 cm

2. 7 in. · 14 in.

3.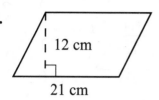

12 cm · 21 cm

_____   _____   _____

Find the area of each parallelogram.

4. $b = 7$ cm
   $h = 9$ cm

5. $b = 12$ m
   $h = 8$ m

6. $b = 21$ in.
   $h = 7$ in.

7. $b = 15$ cm
   $h = 6$ cm

_____   _____   _____   _____

Find the area of each triangle.

8. $b = 16$ cm
   $h = 7$ cm

9. $b = 18$ cm
   $h = 6$ cm

10. $b = 22$ in.
    $h = 9$ in.

11. $b = 4$ ft
    $h = 2\frac{1}{2}$ ft

_____   _____   _____   _____

MIXED APPLICATIONS

12. Abby plants peonies in a triangular garden with a 12-ft base and an $8\frac{1}{2}$-ft. height. If she allows 3 square feet per peony, how many can she plant?

_____

13. A 5-gallon can of asphalt sealant covers about 250 square feet. How many cans of sealant are needed to cover a tennis court that is 78 ft by 27 ft?

_____

NUMBER SENSE

14. A regular hexagon is separated into three congruent rhombuses. Each side of the hexagon is 6 in. long, and the height of the hexagon is 10.4 in. What is the area of the hexagon to the nearest square inch?

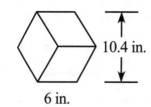

10.4 in.

6 in.

_____

119

Area of Trapezoids

Find each area.

1.

5 m
4 m
12 m

_____

2.

12 cm
12 cm

_____

3.

10 cm
5 cm
6 cm

_____

4.

20 m
15 m

_____

5.
11 m
16 m

_____

6.
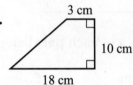
3 cm
10 cm
18 cm

_____

Find the area of each trapezoid.

7. $b_1 = 9$ cm
$b_2 = 11$ cm
$h = 5$ cm

_____

8. $b_1 = 6$ m
$b_2 = 14$ m
$h = 7$ m

_____

9. $b_1 = 24$ cm
$b_2 = 36$ cm
$h = 40$ cm

_____

10. $b_1 = 15$ in.
$b_2 = 6$ in.
$h = 9$ in.

_____

MIXED APPLICATIONS

11. A plaque is shaped like a trapezoid with a
height of 6 in. and bases that measure 3.5 in.
and 9.5 in. What is the area of the plaque?

_____

12. A triangle and a rectangle have equal areas
and the same height of 8 cm. If the base of
the rectangle is 7 cm, how long is the base
of the triangle?

_____

VISUAL THINKING

For Exercises 13–14, the horizontal and vertical distance between two dots represents 1 unit.

13. Locate point *D* and connect dots to form
trapezoid *ABCD* with an area of 10 square units.

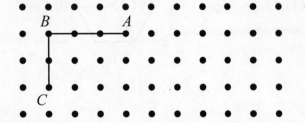

14. Locate point *S* and connect dots to form
trapezoid *PQRS* with an area of 15 square units.

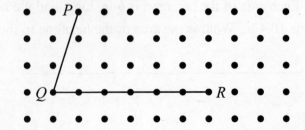

Exploring Area of Irregular Figures

Find the area of familiar shapes in Figure A for Exercises 1–3.

Figure A

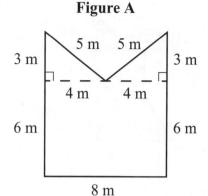

1. Into what familiar shapes does the dashed line divide Figure A?

   _____

2. What is the area of each shape?

   _____

3. What is the area of Figure A? _____

Look at Figure B. Find the area of the shaded part of Figure B.

Figure B

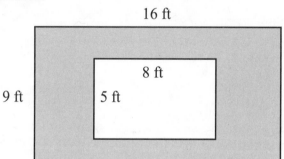

4. What familiar shapes do you see in Figure B? _____

5. How do you find the shaded area of Figure B?

   _____

   _____

6. What is the area of the shaded

   part of Figure B? _____

Find the area of the shaded part of each figure.

7.

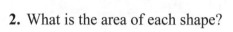

_____

8.

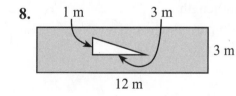

_____

9.

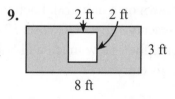

_____

WRITER'S CORNER

10. Explain in your own words when you would use addition to find the area of an irregular figure and when you would use subtraction.

_____

_____

Solving Area Problems

Find the area of each figure. Use 3.14 for π.

1.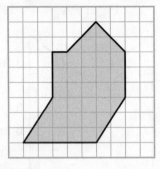

2.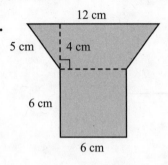

3.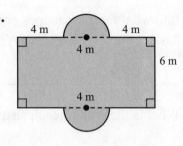

_____   _____   _____

4. Show two different ways to divide the composite figure. Find the area both ways. Show your work below.

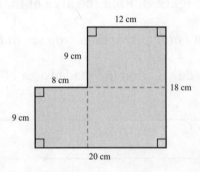

5. Sal is tiling his entryway. The floor plan is drawn on a unit grid. Each unit length represents 1 foot. Tile costs $2.25 per square foot. How much will Sal pay to tile his entryway?

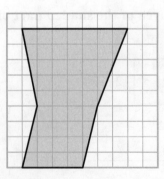

_____

6. A composite figure is formed by combining a square and a triangle. Its total area is 32.5 ft^2. The area of the triangle is 7.5 ft^2. What is the length of each side of the square?

_____

122

Cylinders, Cones, and Spheres

Write *cylinder*, *cone*, or *sphere* to identify each geometric figure. Two views are shown for each figure.

1.

    side view   top view

_____

2.

    top view   side view

_____

3.

    bottom view side view

_____

Write *cylinder*, *cone*, or *sphere* for each description.

4. one curved surface, no flat surfaces

_____

5. one curved surface, one flat surface

_____

Write *cylinder*, *cone*, or *sphere* to identify the described geometric figure or figures. Explain.

6. ideal shape for a pencil

_____

7. ideal shape for a tennis ball

_____

MIXED APPLICATIONS

8. Tammy wants to make a cylindrical container for tennis balls with a diameter equal to 2.5 inches. What is the minimum circumference of a can in which the balls could be stacked on top of each other?

_____

9. A rocket consists of a cylindrical body and a conical top. If the circumference of the base of the cone is 2 inches greater than the 19-inch circumference of the body, what is the radius of the base of the cone?

_____

SCIENCE CONNECTION

Give the circumference of the following. Round your answers to the nearest hundredth.

10. Earth has a radius of 6.36×10^6 m. _____

11. The radius of the moon's orbit around the sun is 3.82×10^8 m. _____

12. The Earth's radius of orbit around the sun is 1.50×10^{11} m. _____

Exploring Three-Dimensional Drawings

Use one-point perspective to draw each view. Do not show hidden lines.

1. Draw a right view.

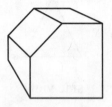

2. Draw a left view.

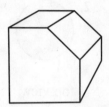

3. Draw a left view.

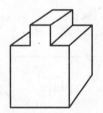

4. Draw a right view.

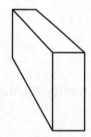

MIXED APPLICATIONS

5. How many cubes with a 1-inch edge are needed to fill a rectangular prism with dimensions 4 inches by 5 inches by 2 inches? to make a cube with a 3-inch edge?

6. After her vacation, Judy wanted to show her teacher a right view of the two L's in the HOLLYWOOD sign in California. Draw the picture for her. Omit hidden lines.

VISUAL THINKING

7. Draw any three-dimensional object from either a left or right perspective. Then try to draw the opposite perspective of your drawing.

Cross Sections

Describe each cross section of the right rectangular prism with the name of its shape.

1.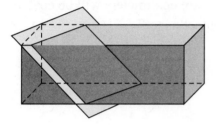

_____

2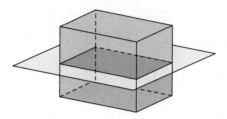

_____

3.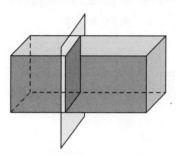

_____

4.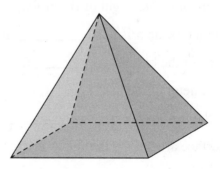

_____

A right rectangular pyramid is shown.

5. The shape of the base is a

_____.

The shape of each side is a

_____.

6. Write the cross sections that are possible.
Write *square*, *rectangle*, *triangle*, *circle*, or *trapezoid*.

_____

VISUAL THINKING

7. What are the three possible cross sections of a cylinder? _____

8. How many possible cross sections are there of a sphere? Name them.

_____

Solving Surface Area Problems

Find the surface area of each figure.

1.

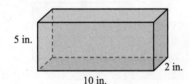

_____

2

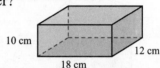

_____

3. Carla is wrapping a present in the box shown below. Find the amount of wrapping paper she needs, not counting overlap.

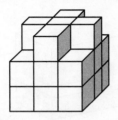

5 in.
2 in.
10 in.

_____

4. Henry plans to cover the box shown below in contact paper without any overlap. How many square centimeters will be covered with contact paper?

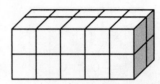

10 cm
12 cm
18 cm

_____

5. To find the surface area of a triangular prism, use the formula $S = 2B + Ph$ where B is the area of the base, P is the perimeter of the bases, and h is the height of the prism.

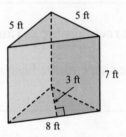

5 ft
5 ft
7 ft
3 ft
8 ft

The height of the prism is _____ ft.

The area of the base is _____ ft^2 .

The perimeter of the base is _____ ft.

Fill in the formula. $S = 2 \cdot$ _____ + _____ × _____

The surface area of the triangular prism is _____ ft^2.

MIXED APPLICATIONS

Find the surface area of each composite figure.

6.

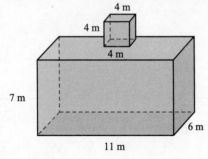

4 m
4 m
4 m
7 m
6 m
11 m

_____

7.

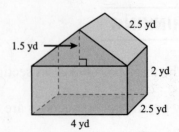

2.5 yd
1.5 yd
2 yd
2.5 yd
4 yd

_____

126

Name _____ Date _____

Surface Area of Prisms

Find the surface area of each figure.

1.
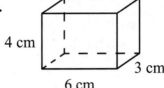

4 cm

6 cm

3 cm

_____

2.
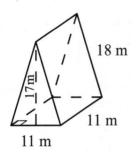

18 m

17 m

11 m

11 m

_____

3.
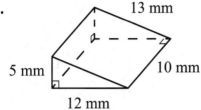

13 mm

5 mm

10 mm

12 mm

_____

4.
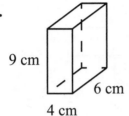

9 cm

6 cm

4 cm

_____

5.

9 m

9 m

9 m

_____

6.
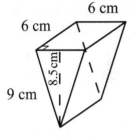

6 cm

6 cm

8.5 cm

9 cm

_____

MIXED APPLICATIONS

7. In an experiment with light, Rodney used 6 square polarized filters 3 in. on a side. What was the total surface area of the filters? Count one face only for each filter.

_____

8. Jane needs to buy insulation for the inside of a truck container. The container is a rectangular prism 15 feet long, 8 feet wide, and 7.5 feet high. How much insulation should Jane buy if all the interior surfaces except the floor are to be insulated?

_____

VISUAL THINKING

9. A large cube is painted blue on all sides and is then cut into 27 congruent cubes. How many of the small cubes are blue

on 3 sides? _____

on 2 sides? _____

on 1 side? _____

on no side? _____

Solving Volume Problems

Find the volume of each figure.

1.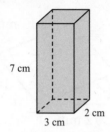

7 cm
3 cm
2 cm

_____

2.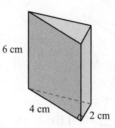

6 cm
4 cm
2 cm

_____

3.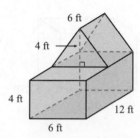

6 ft
4 ft
4 ft
6 ft
12 ft

_____

4. Pete fills the container shown with sand. How much sand fills the container?

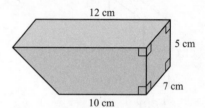

12 cm
5 cm
7 cm
10 cm

_____

5. Mr. Fowler is building a barn for his farm. The dimensions are shown at right. Find the volume of the entire barn.

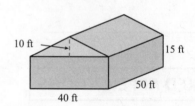

10 ft
15 ft
50 ft
40 ft

_____

6. A movie theater offers popcorn in two different containers for the same price. One container is a rectangular prism with a base area of 36 in.² and a height of 5 in. The other container is a triangular prism with a base area of 32 in.² and a height of 6 in. Which container is the better deal? Explain.

_____

_____

VISUAL THINKING

7. Can rectangular prisms have different heights and the same volume? Draw two examples to explain your answer.

Volume of Prisms

Find the volume of each figure.

1.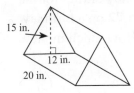
15 in.
12 in.
20 in.

_____

2.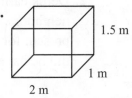
1.5 m
1 m
2 m

_____

3.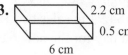
2.2 cm
0.5 cm
6 cm

_____

4.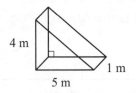
4 m
1 m
5 m

_____

5.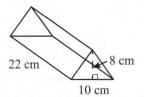
22 cm
8 cm
10 cm

_____

6.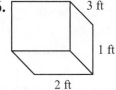
3 ft
1 ft
2 ft

_____

Find the volume of the shaded portion of each figure.

7.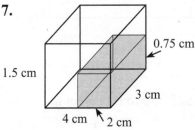
0.75 cm
1.5 cm
3 cm
4 cm
2 cm

_____

8.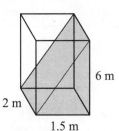
6 m
2 m
1.5 m

_____

9.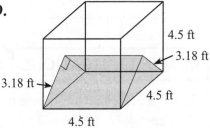
4.5 ft
3.18 ft
3.18 ft
4.5 ft
4.5 ft

_____

MIXED APPLICATIONS

10. A box has a volume of 1,000 cm³. If the box is a cube, what are its dimensions?

_____

11. The cargo-carrying part of Billy's truck is a rectangular prism with a length of 8.3 m, a width of 3 m, and a height of 4.2 m. What is the maximum volume of sand that Billy's truck can carry?

_____

LOGICAL REASONING

12. How can you quickly determine the surface area of a cube?

_____

Using Addition and Subtraction

Estimate each answer. Then find each answer.

1. Maria bought a new bicycle for $126.45. She paid $4.94 in sales tax. How much did Maria pay for the new bicycle in all?

   _____

2. Derek earned $10.00 baby-sitting for his neighbors. He spent $5.72 on a birthday present for his sister. How much money did he have left?

   _____

3. Individual times for the relay team in minutes were 1.05, 1.12, 1.07, and 1.02. Find the total time for the relay team.

   _____

4. The Amazon River is 6,411 kilometers long. The Mississippi River is 6,234 kilometers long. How much longer is the Amazon than the Mississippi?

   _____

5. A theater received $382.50, $411.75, and $243.00 from ticket sales on three evenings last weekend. How much did the theater receive in all for those evenings?

   _____

6. Tokyo is 11,532 miles from Rio de Janeiro and 6,053 miles from Paris. How much farther is Tokyo from Rio de Janeiro than it is from Paris?

   _____

MIXED APPLICATIONS

7. Ian received an allowance of $30.00. He spent $4.77, $6.96, and $14.29 for CDs. How much of his allowance remained?

   _____

8. Polly has saved $255.50 to buy a computer that costs $799.95. Her parents give her $145.00. How much more must Polly save before she can buy the computer?

   _____

EVERYDAY MATH CONNECTION

To record banking transactions in a checkbook, you add deposits and subtract checks. Find each final balance.

9. Balance: $780.42
   Deposit: $66.50
   Check: $347.95
   Final Balance: _____

10. Balance: $1,021.65
    Deposit: $590.89
    Check: $482.44
    Final Balance: _____

Problem Solving

MULTISTEP PROBLEMS

Write the steps for solving each problem.

1. The eighth-grade students are selling magazine subscriptions to raise money for a class trip. They earn $3 for every subscription they sell. So far, they have earned $228 of the $396 needed. How many more subscriptions must the students sell to meet their goal?

_____

_____

2. On their vacation, the Li family traveled from their home to a resort in the mountains. The odometer in their car read 35286.9 miles when they started and 35514.2 miles when they returned home. What was the distance from their home to the resort?

_____

_____

3. Geraldo bought some computer software on layaway. He paid $12 down and must make a payment of $5 each week for 4 weeks. How much will Geraldo pay in all?

_____

_____

4. Mrs. Bond made a deposit of $100 into her checking account. Then she wrote checks for $97.54 and $48.27. If her previous balance was $320.39, what is her new balance?

_____

_____

MIXED APPLICATIONS

5. Mikhail bought two copies of the same book and a tape priced at $11.95. He gave the cashier $60 and received $4.27 in change. How much did each book cost?

_____

6. Rhoda had $478.40 in her checking account. She wrote one check for $31.75 and another check for $85.50. Then she made a deposit of $150.00. What was her new balance?

_____

WRITER'S CORNER

7. Write a word problem that has more than one step in the solution.

_____

_____

131

Using Multiplication and Division

Solve each problem.

1. On each of 26 trips to a national park in June, a sightseeing bus carried a full load of 28 passengers. How many passengers did the bus carry in June?

_____

2. The driver of a sightseeing bus put 25 gallons of gasoline into the bus. The gasoline cost $3.31 per gallon. What was the total cost of the gasoline?

_____

3. An office paid $389.40 for 12 temporary workers for 1 day of work. Each worker was paid the same amount of money. How much did each worker receive?

_____

4. A police department bought 16 new cars. The department paid a total of $164,797.12 for the cars. What was the average cost of each car?

_____

5. Pam paid $8.75 per day to rent a VCR. She rented the recorder for 11 days. How much did she pay in all?

_____

6. Mary pays $0.95 per bag of ice for a party. Her bill for ice is $27.55. How many bags of ice does Mary buy?

_____

MIXED APPLICATIONS

7. Mr. and Mrs. Rappold plan to stay at a certain hotel for five nights. They can pay $72.26 per night, single occupancy, plus $10.00 per night for each additional person. Or, they can pay $380.00 for 5 nights with no restrictions. Which option will cost the Rappolds less money?

_____

8. Brian bought some dog food for $0.57 per can and some cat food for $0.75 per can. He paid $5.85 for a total of 9 cans of pet food. How many cans of dog food did he buy?

_____

NUMBER SENSE

Find the missing numbers.

9.
```
  [ ] , 7  1  5
    4 , 2  1  8
  + 1 , 6  2 [ ]
  ─────────────
    9 , [ ] 6  0
```

10.
```
  [ ]  7 , [ ] 3 [ ]
  - [ ] , 2 [ ] 6
  ─────────────────
    8 , 9  3  9
```

Problem-Solving Strategies

MAKING DECISIONS

Gina LaRosa needs a new dress for the high school prom. Gina and her family are considering the following options.

Option A: Gina can buy a formal that costs $250.

Option B: Gina can rent a formal for $75.

Option C: Mrs. LaRosa can take 4 hours off from her work and make a dress. She earns $20 per hour, which she would lose by not working. She would need to buy 8 yards of material for the dress at $7.50 per yard, a pattern for $4.95, and other items for $9.45.

1. How much in earnings would Mrs. LaRosa lose by making the dress?

_____

2. How much would Option C cost the LaRosa family?

_____

3. Find the difference in cost between Option A and Option C and between Option C and Option B.

_____

4. Which option do you think the LaRosa family should choose? Give reasons for your answer.

_____

_____

MIXED APPLICATIONS

5. Mrs. Dunkelman works as a freelance artist. She earns $20.25 per hour. Last week she worked 39 hours. About how much did she earn last week?

_____

6. The price of a framed picture is $28 less than twice the price of an unframed picture. The price of a framed picture is $70. What is the price of an unframed picture?

_____

133

Problem Solving

MULTISTEP PROBLEMS

1. Inés paid $36 for swimming lessons. Each lesson lasted $\frac{3}{4}$ hour and cost $4. How many hours of swimming lessons did she have?

_____

2. Last month Hilary played 15 games of tennis. She won 3 more games than she lost. Keith won $1\frac{1}{3}$ times the number of games that Hilary won. How many games did Keith win?

_____

MIXED APPLICATIONS

3. Dennis rode his bicycle around a circular path $4\frac{1}{2}$ miles long. He started at the gate house and rode 7 miles in a clockwise direction before he stopped for a rest. How far did he have to go to reach the gate house again?

_____

4. A farmer has 600 feet of wire to make a fence for one side of his garden. The fence will have 3 strands of wire attached to posts 8 feet apart. How many fence posts will be needed?

_____

LOGICAL REASONING

5. The numbers in each box have separate patterns across and down. Look for the patterns and fill in the missing numbers.

$\frac{5}{4}$		5	10
		1	2
		$\frac{1}{5}$	$\frac{2}{5}$
$\frac{1}{100}$			$\frac{2}{25}$

6. Describe any patterns you see along the diagonals of the boxes for Exercise 5.

_____

_____

_____

Name _____ Date _____

Problem-Solving Strategies

CHOOSE A STRATEGY

Solve.

1. The Moros have a rectangular swimming pool in the center of their backyard. The backyard is $60\frac{1}{4}$ ft long and $32\frac{1}{2}$ ft wide. The pool is 35 ft long and $12\frac{3}{4}$ ft wide. How many feet does the yard extend beyond each side of the pool?

2. Lee needs 32 sections of fencing for the backyard. The fence will be in the shape of a rectangle. If 12 sections are needed for each long side, how many sections are in each width?

3. From her home Rhonda jogged 3 blocks north, 4 blocks east, 2 blocks north, 1 block east, 5 blocks south, and 3 blocks west. How many blocks from home was she?

4. Clint roped 53 cows this week. This is 9 more than the number of cows he roped last week. How many cows did he rope last week?

5. Abdul wants to hang a square poster that measures $1\frac{1}{2}$ feet on a side in the center of a 12-foot-long wall. How far from the end of the wall should Abdul place the side of the poster?

6. Jamie gave Fawn $0.95 in dimes and nickels. There were 5 more dimes than nickels. How many of each coin were there?

7. Rick works part-time at a bicycle shop. He worked for $3\frac{1}{5}$ hours on Monday, $2\frac{1}{2}$ hours on Tuesday, and $4\frac{3}{4}$ hours on Wednesday. About how many hours did he work in the three days?

8. Binti saved $3 this week. Suppose she doubles the amount of her savings each week for the next 4 weeks. What total amount will she save during the 5 weeks?

Problem-Solving Strategies

FIND A PATTERN

1. The number of students at Jefferson High School has been decreasing steadily from 911 two years ago to 862 last year to 813 today. If the trend continues, how many students will be at Jefferson High School next year?

_____

2. Leonard's hourly wage has increased steadily every 6 months. It has gone from $16.50 per hour to $17.25 per hour to $18.00 per hour. If the pattern continues, how much will he make in another 6 months?

_____

3. Suppose one day a person gave a card to six friends. Suppose the next day each of the six friends gave a card to six of their friends and so on. How many people will receive a card on the fourth day?

_____

4. Suppose that nine 9s are multiplied together.
$9 \times 9 \times 9 \times 9 \times 9 \times 9 \times 9 \times 9 \times 9$
What is the ones digit of the answer? (HINT: Multiply two nines together; three nines; four nines. Look for a pattern in the ones digit.)

_____

5. Devante wrote the following number pattern: 0.00054, 0.0054, 0.054. Write the next number in the pattern as a number between 1 and 10 times a power of 10 (scientific notation).

_____

6. Luciana had 3 employees in 2007. Her business grew to 9 employees in 2008. Then there were 27 employees in 2009. At this growth rate, how many employees were there in 2011?

_____

Answer Key

Page 1

1. 1,171
2. 234
3. 23.64
4. 668.61
5. 69.11
6. 62.95
7. 27.5
8. 35.29
9. 442.3
10. 1.3222
11. 731.98
12. 63.036
13. 38.6
14. 262.434
15. Unnex: 7,640 sq mi; Biron: 6,680 sq mi
16. $2, $4, $8, $16
17. 57; The two numbers in each pair have a sum of 10, or 100, or 1,000, and so on.

Page 2

1. 0.27
2. 0.375
3. 0.08750
4. 540.0
5. 42.200
6. 21.0684
7. 0.162225
8. 0.04872
9. 0.36
10. 0.24
11. 0.049
12. 0.1395
13. 72.00
14. 0.0060
15. 7.128
16. 5.22
17. 0.4165
18. 0.06650
19. 0.6474
20. 34.0545
21. 409 mph
22. $224.50
23. 222,222; 333,333; 56

Page 3

1. 227.65
2. 320
3. 733.5
4. 417,600.

5–20. Estimates may vary.

5. [2] 1.9
6. [15] 13
7. [30] 30
8. [1] 1.2
9. [3] 3.1
10. [7] 7.2
11. [40] 41
12. [12] 12.2
13. [3] 3.3
14. [75] 69
15. [40] 42
16. [100] 90
17. [30] 29.3
18. [150] 154
19. [90] 86.31
20. [30] 32.9
21. 23
22. 23
23. 23
24. 230
25. 230
26. 0.23
27. 1.5
28. 34.5
29. 0.45; 0.09

Page 4

1–20. Estimates may vary.

1. [15] 15.2
2. [3] 3.19
3. [15] 15
4. [600] 606
5. [5] 5.1
6. [50] 52.5
7. [4] 5.06
8. [80] 68
9. [2] 2
10. [8] 8
11. [6] 7
12. [5] 5.4
13. [3] 2.9
14. [0.5] 0.5
15. [2] 2.16
16. [3] 3.28
17. [128] 136.17
18. [2] 1.967
19. [0.5] 0.485
20. [2] 1.538
21. 3.5; 0.35
22. 146.42; 14.642
23. about 16.5 mm
24. about $2.50
25. 200; 8

Page 5

1. 24 years old
2. Possible answer: 5 pennies, 8 nickels, 2 dimes
3. 3 times
4. 20
5. $4
6. Addie, 4 oz; Blissy, 14 oz; Corky, 8 oz
7. 3: 3; 4: 3 + 1; 5: 9 − 3 − 1; 6: 9 − 3; 7: 9 − 3 + 1; 8: 9 − 1; 9: 9; 10: 9 + 1; 11: 9 + 3 − 1; 12: 9 + 3; 13: 9 + 3 + 1

Page 6

1. Answers will vary. Possible answer: The random sample, because it is more likely to represent adults whose interests are varied.
2. data, predict
3. survey
4. random
5. <
6. <
7. >
8. >
9. <
10. =

Page 7

1. 16; 21; 33
2. about 129 students
3. about 202 students
4. about 18 students
5. about 95 students
6. 2 student tickets
7. 8 ways; for SHOW, 2 choices from each letter on row 2, or 4 in all; then 2 choices from each of those choices, or 8 in all.
8. 16 ways; for DANCE, same as SHOW, then 2 choices from each of the 8, or 16 in all.

137

Page 8

1–2. Answers will vary.

1. Paul's sample was biased. Maybe his friends studied more than other students.

2. Nancy did not average as many stations, and the report could include stations nationwide, while Nancy's statistics are very local.

3. It is a biased sample because it does not include girls.

4. It is biased because it includes only students that picked band as their elective class.

5. 48 people

6. 13 boxes

Page 9

1. seventh grade; 20 more students

2. eighth grade; 3 greater

3. mean, 21; median, 24; mode, 12

4. mean, 28; median, 32; no mode

5. 8 boxes

6. 11 minutes

7. Ann and Doris

Page 10

1. 75.71; 75; 75 and 80

2. 5.76; 5.12; no mode

3. 5 lb; 5 lb; no mode

4. 29; 25; 25

5. 75, 80

6. 75

7. false

8. false

9. 21 hours

10. 3; 3; 3

11. Check problem.

Page 11

1.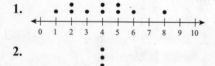

2.

3. 4; 1.6

4. 3.8; 0.68

5–6. Answers will vary.

5. The average is 4, but the number of people varies greatly. You might infer that the population lives in many different sizes of homes.

6. The average is 3.8, and the MAD is small. These people might all live in the same neighborhood.

7. 11.2; 3.44

8. Find the mean of each list.

Page 12

1–13. Estimates may vary.

1. $[\frac{1}{2}]$ $\frac{4}{9}$

2. $[1]$ $1\frac{1}{8}$

3. $[0]$ $\frac{1}{8}$

4. $[\frac{1}{2}]$ $\frac{1}{2}$

5. $[1]$ $\frac{11}{12}$

6. $[1\frac{1}{2}]$ $1\frac{3}{10}$

7. $[0]$ $\frac{1}{12}$

8. $[2]$ $1\frac{7}{12}$

9. $[\frac{1}{2}]$ $\frac{11}{24}$

10. $[1\frac{1}{2}]$ $1\frac{7}{20}$

11. $[1]$ $1\frac{1}{12}$

12. $[2]$ $1\frac{17}{24}$

13. $[0]$ $\frac{4}{25}$

14. $\frac{1}{3}$

15. 45 DVDs

16–19. Answers will vary

16. 1, 2, 1

17. 1, 1, 3

18. 1, 1, 7

19. 3, 1, 1

Page 13

1. 11

2. $8\frac{1}{3}$

3. $19\frac{1}{5}$

4. $9\frac{3}{4}$

5. $12\frac{1}{2}$

6. $25\frac{1}{4}$

7. $7\frac{5}{6}$

8. $25\frac{7}{24}$

9. $10\frac{1}{3}$

10. $12\frac{13}{15}$

11. $22\frac{5}{12}$

12. $21\frac{9}{40}$

13. $7\frac{7}{12}$

14. $10\frac{7}{40}$

15. $14\frac{26}{35}$

16. $9\frac{5}{8}$

17. 19

18. $18\frac{1}{2}$

19. $16\frac{4}{5}$

20. $7\frac{5}{24}$

21. $51\frac{1}{3}$ yd

22. $\frac{1}{6}, \frac{1}{3}, \frac{1}{2}$

23. $\frac{1}{6}, \frac{1}{4}, \frac{1}{3}$

Page 14

1. $\frac{3}{5}$

2. $\frac{10}{15} = \frac{2}{3}$

3. $\frac{7}{8}$

4. $\frac{5}{6}$

5. $\frac{25}{36}$

6. $19\frac{5}{8}$

7. $7\frac{19}{20}$

8. $5\frac{10}{9} = 6\frac{1}{9}$

9. $11\frac{13}{20}$

10. $10\frac{13}{15}$

11. $3\frac{19}{20}$

12. $17\frac{5}{8}$

13. $\frac{17}{15} = 1\frac{2}{15}$

14. $\frac{7}{18}$

15. $13\frac{13}{14}$

16. $15\frac{5}{6}$ hr

17. $763\frac{7}{20}$ gal

18. Possible answers: $\frac{3}{4} = \frac{1}{2} + \frac{1}{4}$; $\frac{8}{15} = \frac{1}{3} + \frac{1}{5}$; $\frac{7}{12} = \frac{1}{4} + \frac{1}{3}$; $\frac{2}{3} = \frac{1}{2} + \frac{1}{6}$, $\frac{1}{2} = \frac{1}{3} + \frac{1}{6}$

Page 15

1. $6\frac{1}{3}$

2. $11\frac{2}{5}$

3. $2\frac{1}{2}$

4. $8\frac{1}{3}$

5. $7\frac{5}{8}$

6. $7\frac{1}{6}$

7. $13\frac{3}{10}$

8. $8\frac{7}{16}$

9. $4\frac{2}{3}$

10. $3\frac{1}{3}$

11. $1\frac{5}{6}$

12. $8\frac{5}{8}$

13. $6\frac{1}{2}$

14. $\frac{3}{8}$

15. $2\frac{1}{2}$

16. $11\frac{1}{6}$

17. $\frac{3}{4}$

18. $3\frac{7}{10}$

19. $\frac{3}{4}$ hr

20. $1\frac{1}{12}$ hr

21. One possible answer:

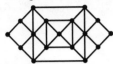

Page 16

1. $\frac{2}{7}$

2. $\frac{5}{36}$

3. $\frac{31}{60}$

4. $6\frac{7}{18}$

5. $4\frac{5}{8}$

6. 3

7. 3

8. $\frac{7}{10}$

9. $\frac{3}{8}$

10. $8\frac{1}{24}$

11. $\frac{5}{12}$

12. 1

13. $69\frac{1}{30}$ hr

14. $\frac{1}{4}$

15. $<$

16. $>$

17. $>$

18. $=$

19–22. Estimates will vary.

19. 11,000

20. 6

21. 12

22. $\frac{1}{2}$

Page 17

1. $\frac{1}{8}$

2. $\frac{2}{5}$

3. $\frac{5}{14}$

4. $\frac{1}{4}$

5. $\frac{7}{16}$

6. $\frac{8}{35}$

7. $\frac{1}{7}$

8. $\frac{1}{2}$

9. $\frac{1}{5}$

10. $\frac{1}{9}$

11. $\frac{3}{4}$

12. $\frac{7}{24}$

13. $>$

14. $<$

15. $=$

16. $=$

17. $<$

18. $=$

19. $\frac{1}{4}$

20. $\frac{1}{5}$

21. 8 carnations, 12 zinnias

22. 4, 6

23. 5, 9

Page 18

1. $\frac{1}{4}$ and $\frac{4}{1}$; $\frac{2}{5}$ and $\frac{5}{2}$

2. $\frac{2}{3}$ and $\frac{3}{2}$; $\frac{1}{9}$ and $\frac{9}{1}$

3. 1

4. $\frac{7}{9}$

5. $\frac{7}{48}$

6. 1

7. 9

8. $\frac{25}{16}$ or $1\frac{9}{16}$

9. $\frac{3}{4}$

10. $\frac{7}{10}$

11. $\frac{4}{21}$

12. 1

13. $\frac{11}{90}$

14. $\frac{3}{8}$

15. $\frac{5}{24}$

16. $\frac{4}{5}$

17. 8 palm trees

18. $\frac{11}{12}$ of the garden

19. $\frac{1}{25}$

20. $\frac{4}{9}$

21. $\frac{8}{125}$

22. $\frac{1}{27}$

Page 19

1. 18

2. 15

3. $5\frac{2}{3}$

4. 39

5. $1\frac{1}{8}$

6. 10

7. 15

8. $8\frac{1}{3}$

9. $2\frac{1}{4}$

10. $12\frac{4}{5}$

11. $6\frac{1}{2}$

12. $1\frac{3}{7}$

13. $7\frac{1}{5}$

14. 21

15. 60

16. 2

17. $2\frac{4}{5}$

18. $\frac{2}{9}$

19. $22\frac{1}{2}$

20. $\frac{1}{12}$

21. $\frac{1}{10}$

22. 15, 18

23. 20, 24

24. 35, 40

Page 20

1. 45

2. $\frac{44}{45}$

3. $\frac{36}{11}$ or $3\frac{3}{11}$

4. $18\frac{2}{3}$

5. 26

6. $6\frac{1}{3}$

7. $34\frac{2}{3}$

8. $35\frac{13}{20}$

9. $34\frac{3}{8}$

10. $1\frac{5}{16}$

11. $1\frac{83}{160}$

12. 0.25 or $\frac{1}{4}$

13. 0.375 or $\frac{3}{8}$

14. 4.275 or $4\frac{11}{40}$

15. Possible answers: $2\frac{1}{2} \times 3\frac{3}{20}$, $1\frac{1}{2} \times 5\frac{1}{4}$

16. $27\frac{1}{2}$ lb

17. $9\frac{27}{32}$ hr

18–25. Estimates may vary.

18. 1,800

19. 104

20. 1

21. 40

22. 1.5

23. 32

24. 2

25. 77

139

Page 21

1. 4
2. 8
3. 9
4. 3
5. 9
6. 4
7. $7\frac{1}{2}$
8. $3\frac{1}{3}$
9. 6
10. 8
11. 5
12. 6
13. 20
14. 3
15. ▓▓▓░

Page 22

1. 7
2. $\frac{1}{6}$
3. $\frac{8}{9}$
4. $\frac{3}{10}$
5. $\frac{4}{9}$
6. $\frac{5}{2}$
7. 12
8. 21
9. $2\frac{2}{5}$
10. 3
11. $\frac{1}{2}$
12. 16
13. $1\frac{1}{4}$
14. $\frac{5}{8}$
15. $1\frac{3}{4}$
16. $2\frac{2}{3}$
17. 7
18. $\frac{3}{4}$
19. $\frac{2}{7}$
20. 6
21. $\frac{1}{10}$
22. 5
23. 10
24. 8
25. 17 times
26. 30 books
27. $1\frac{9}{40}$
28. $1\frac{9}{20}$
29. $10\frac{5}{8}$
30. $4\frac{8}{9}$
31. $\frac{13}{24}$
32. $\frac{4}{35}$

Page 23

1. $\frac{5}{4}$ or $1\frac{1}{4}$
2. 10
3. $\frac{119}{108}$ or $1\frac{11}{108}$
4. $\frac{1}{10}$
5. $\frac{115}{72}$ or $1\frac{43}{72}$
6. $1\frac{7}{8}$
7. $\frac{10}{81}$
8. $\frac{1}{45}$
9. 16
10. $\frac{1}{48}$
11. $\frac{10}{13}$
12. $\frac{27}{50}$
13. $\frac{1}{6}$
14. $\frac{22}{15}$ or $1\frac{7}{15}$
15. 8 boards; no
16. $4\frac{3}{4}$ cars
17. $\frac{3}{8} \div \frac{1}{4} = 1\frac{1}{2}$
18. $24 \div \frac{4}{9} = 54$
19. $\frac{4}{9} \div \frac{2}{7} = 1\frac{5}{9}$
20. $\frac{2}{3} \div \frac{6}{7} = \frac{7}{9}$
21. $10 \div \frac{5}{12} = 24$
22. $\frac{8}{13} \div \frac{2}{7} = 2\frac{2}{13}$

Page 24

1. $\frac{1}{15}$
2. $2\frac{2}{3}$
3. $8\frac{1}{2}$
4. $\frac{2}{7}$
5. $\frac{2}{3}$
6. $1\frac{1}{2}$
7. 5
8. 9
9. $10\frac{1}{2}$
10. $\frac{3}{4}$
11. $\frac{1}{5}$
12. $7\frac{1}{5}$
13. 6
14. $9\frac{2}{5}$
15. 33
16. 4
17. $8\frac{4}{5}$
18. $4\frac{1}{2}$
19. $2\frac{2}{3}$
20. 14
21. $\frac{3}{8}$

22. $4\frac{1}{2}$
23. $\frac{1}{8}$
24. $2\frac{2}{3}$
25. $1\frac{1}{3}$
26. $13\frac{1}{3}$
27. $3\frac{1}{2}$
28. 12 days
29. 9 oz
30. 2, 3

Page 25

1. $2\frac{7}{10}$
2. $\frac{23}{24}$
3. $\frac{1}{15}$
4. $2\frac{1}{4}$
5. $4\frac{1}{8}$
6. $4\frac{1}{2}$
7. $\frac{2}{9}$
8. $\frac{25}{184}$
9. $\frac{2}{11}$
10. $\frac{153}{82}$ or $1\frac{71}{82}$
11. $\frac{1}{2}$
12. $1\frac{1}{5}$
13. $\frac{3}{5}$
14. $4\frac{14}{15}$
15. $2\frac{11}{32}$
16. 6 servings
17. $1\frac{2}{3}$ ft
18. =
19. ≠
20. =
21. ≠
22. Multiplication is associative; division is not.

Page 26

1. $6.9x + 3.3$
2. $4x - 4$
3. $x + \frac{1}{2}$
4. $5x + 15$
5. Joey: $20; Julie: $20; total: $40
6. $210
7. $\frac{1}{4}(4 \times 6 + 4 \times 9)$
8. $24 + 36x$
9. $5x - 25$
10. $12x + 10$
11. $10x - 60$
12. $7; y$
13. $3; z; 4$

140

Page 27

1. 42; s; 42; s; 0.42s; 0.42s; $s +$ 0.42s; 1.42s
2. Possible answer: The expression with two terms shows the original cost and the markup. One term allows for quicker calculation, and it shows that increasing the cost by 42% is the same as multiplying by 1.42.
3. The expression would change to $1s + 0.34s$ or $1.34s$.
4. $1c + 0.1c$; $1.1c$
5. $1p - 0.05p$; $0.95p$; $14.25

Page 28

1. $c + 2$
2. $c + 2 = 9$
3. 7 cubes
4. 7 cubes
5. 7
6. Remove 3 cubes from each side.
7. $x = 12$
8. $c = 7$
9. $a = 3$
10. Answers will vary. Possible response: The hidden cubes plus 3 cubes on the left pan must balance with 8 cubes on the right pan.

Page 29

1. add -5
2. subtract 5
3. divide by 3
4. divide by -8
5. multiply by 3
6. subtract -6
7. $n = 6$
8. $x = 3$
9. $y = -12$
10. $t = 14$
11. $y = -3$
12. $a = 9$
13. $c = -8$
14. $y = 3$
15. $r = -7$
16. $x = -3$
17. $z = -7$
18. $t = 3$
19. 222 people
20. 9
21. 4th floor

Page 30

1. $x = 12$
2. $x = 4$
3. $x = 99$
4. $x = 6$
5. $x = -18$
6. $x = -5$
7. $2
8. 108 books
9. 84
10. 7 hours
11. 8 laps
12. 14 stickers
13. 10 cm

Page 31

1. 10% or more
2. $152.20
3. $4\frac{1}{4}$ inches
4. $29\frac{1}{8}$ yards
5. at least $33,360
6. $51.04
7. 373 students
8. at least 7.4%

Page 32

1. $4 + c < 11$
2. Remove 4 cubes from each side.
3. $c < 7$
4. Remove 7 cubes from each side.
5. $y < 4$
6. $n > 2$
7. $z < 5$
8. $<$
9. $>$
10. $<$
11. 11.2
12. 0.25
13. 4.2
14. 0.0082
15. 3.358

Page 33

1. $a < 5$; 0, 1, 2, 3, 4
2. $b \leq 7$; 0, 1, 2, 3, 4, 5, 6, 7
3. $c \geq 7$: 7, 8, 9, …
4. $d > 4$; 5, 6, 7, …
5. $k \geq 9$; 9, 10, 11, …
6. $x < 3$; 0, 1, 2
7. $n \neq 3$; all whole numbers except 3
8. $5 > y$; 0, 1, 2, 3, 4
9. $p \geq 13$; 13, 14, 15, …
10. $a - 30 < 450$; $a < 480$; less than $480

11. $6w < 828$; $w < 138$; no, each was paid less than $138.
12. False; "more than 12" means 13, 14, 15, …
13. Cannot tell; the total number of games played is not given.

Page 34

1–9. Check graphs.
1. $a < -1$
2. $b > 14$
3. $c < 1.5$
4. $d \geq 10$
5. $e < 5$
6. $t > -7$
7. $t \leq -0.75$
8. $y > -2$
9. $s < 6$
10. $2n - 40 < 120$; $n < 80$; fewer than 80 were sold in April and fewer than 40 in May.
11. $16\frac{1}{3}$ mi
12. $\frac{3}{8}$
13. $-3\frac{4}{7}$
14. $\frac{5}{36}$
15. 12
16. -109
17. 10

Page 35

1. $x \geq -4$
2. $x < -4$
3. $x < 12$
4. $x \leq 4$
5. $\frac{b}{6} \geq 14$; $b \geq 84$; Karen has at least 84 books.
6. The student did not reverse the inequality symbol. The answer should be $x < -45$.
7. $4x < 16$; $x < 4$; the cost of each smoothie was less than $4.
8. The solution set is graphed as a solid line because the cost of each smoothie can be any amount, not just whole number amounts.
9. Each smoothie must cost more than $0; prices are not negative so it does not make sense for a smoothie to be $0 or less.
10.

141

Page 36

1. $x \geq -1$
2. $x < -12\frac{1}{3}$
3. $x \geq 7$
4. $x > -20$
5. $x \leq 12$
6. $x > -4.42$
7. $x \geq -11$;

-12 -11 -10 -9 -8 -7 -6 -5 -4 -3 -2 -1 0

8. $-108 > y$;

-113 -112 -111 -110 -109 -108 -107

9. She can buy at most 5 bagels. The answer to the inequality is 5.83, but since you cannot buy part of a bagel, she can buy at most 5 bagels.
10.

-2 -1 0 1 2 3 4 5

11. $50 + 20x \leq 200$; $x \leq 7$; 7 shirts
12. $90 + 15x \leq 7.33$; no she can afford to buy only 7.3 short-sleeve shirts and since she cannot buy part of a shirt, she can buy at most 7.

Page 37

1. 50°
2. 130°
3. 40°
4. $\angle A$ and $\angle R$
5. $\angle A$ and $\angle M$
6. obtuse
7. acute
8. right
9. acute
10. obtuse
11. right
12–13. Check drawings.
14. No. If $\angle F$ were acute, $\angle D$ would be obtuse, and an obtuse angle cannot be one of a complementary pair.

Page 38

1. 15°
2. 123°
3. $x = 54°$, $y = 126°$, $z = 54°$
4–7. Check drawings.
4. 60°, 150°
5. 5°, 95°
6. 65°, 155°
7. 12°, 102°
8. $m\angle 4 = 107°$, $m\angle 6 = 73°$, $m\angle 5 = 107°$

9. Possible answers are: $\angle 7$, $\angle 1$; $\angle 2$, $\angle 8$; $\angle 3$, $\angle 5$; $\angle 4$, $\angle 6$; $\angle 3$, $\angle 4$; $\angle 5$, $\angle 6$
10. true

Page 39

1. 10°; 100°
2. 65°; 155°
3. 22°; 112°
4. 47°; 137°
5. $\angle BEF$
6. 150°
7. $\angle DBC$
8. $\angle A$
9. $\angle EFD$ and $\angle BFC$; $\angle EFB$ and $\angle DFC$
10. 120°; 240°
11. 160°
12. 70°, 30°; Accept any reasonable drawings.

Page 40

1. 90°
2–5. Answers will vary. Possible answers are given.
2. $\angle SUR$ and $\angle QUR$
3. $\angle SUR$ and $\angle PUQ$
4. $\angle SUR$ and $\angle SUP$
5. 90°; $m\angle SUT = 90°$ and $\angle SUT$ and $\angle NUQ$ are vertical angles. Vertical angles have the same measure.
6. 158°
7. 21°
8. 42; 126°
9. Yes, a parking lot can be built because the measure of angle J is 40°, which is greater than 38°.
10. When two angle measures add up to 180°, the angles are supplementary, not complementary. Complementary angles add up to 90°.

Page 41

1. obtuse
2. right
3. acute
4. acute
5. right
6. right
7. obtuse
8. right
9. acute

10. right
11. obtuse
12. acute
13. isosceles
14. scalene
15. isosceles
16. scalene
17. isosceles
18. equilateral
19. 100°, 50°
20. 12 posts
21.

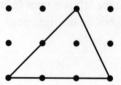

Page 42

1–7. Check constructions.
8. 110°, 70°
9. 0, 5

Page 43

1–7. Check constructions.
5. equilateral
6. isosceles
7. scalene
8. 25°, 65°
9. 14
10. Check drawing. One of the three possible triangles is shown.

Page 44

1. Check drawings. The given conditions will make a unique triangle.
2. no triangle; one; one; no triangle
3. Answers will vary. Possible answer: Yes, I can draw several triangles of different sizes that have 30°, 60°, and 90° angles.
4. No, several differently sized triangles can be drawn with the same angles.
5. Check drawings. Possible answer: Since a triangle has 180°, I drew angles that were about 60° and then connected them with lines that were about the same length.

Page 45

1. $\frac{4}{9}$
2. $\frac{12}{17}$
3. $\frac{5}{8}$
4. $\frac{53}{100}$
5. $\frac{3}{7}$
6. $\frac{3}{5}$
7. $\frac{8}{15}$
8. $\frac{1}{4}$
9. yes
10. no
11. yes
12. no
13. $=$
14. $\neq$
15. $\neq$
16. $=$
17. $\neq$
18. $\neq$
19. $=$
20. $=$
21. $\frac{\$0.10}{1 \text{ apple}}$
22. $\frac{\$0.05}{1 \text{ oz of cereal}}$
23. $\frac{\$13}{1 \text{ dinner}}$
24. 16 oz water
25. $\frac{11}{34}$
26. $\frac{1}{4}$
27. $\frac{2}{3}$
28. $\frac{1}{2}$

Page 46

1. 28, 28, yes
2. 16, 12, no
3. yes; $28 = 28$
4. no; $16 \neq 12$
5. $10y = 5 \times 4$
6. $24n = 18 \times 4$
7. Divide each side by 10 in Exercise 5 and by 24 in Exercise 6.
8. $1 \times 8 = 2 \times 4$
9. $5 \times 12 = 15 \times 4$
10. $6y = 18 \times 1$
11. $12x = 9 \times 8$
12. yes
13. yes
14. no
15. yes
16. no
17. yes
18. yes
19. no
20. 8:3

Page 47

1. $x = 4$
2. $c = 81$
3. $k = 2.5$
4. $a = 8$
5. $y = 20$
6. $h = 8$
7. $z = 12$
8. $d = 2$
9. $c = 5$
10. $n = 9$
11. $b = 24$
12. $e = 5$
13. $n = 16$
14. $n = 21$
15. $n = 30$
16. $n = 5$
17. $n = 9$
18. $n = 15$
19. $n = 7.5$
20. $n = 12$
21. $x = 2\frac{2}{3}$
22. $x = 9$
23. $x = 39$
24. 3 rooms
25. 16 boys
26. $\frac{1}{2}$

Page 48

1. proportional; 60
2. not proportional
3. proportional; 3
4. proportional; 8
5. x is number of hours; y is miles driven; $y = 65x$
6. x is number of ounces; y is milligrams of calcium; $y = 3.9x$
7. x is gallons of gasoline; y is total cost; $y = 3.15x$
8. x is cups of batter; y is number of muffins; $y = 2.5x$
9. $y = 18.5x$
10. $22.50

Page 49

1. 9, 195, 325, 650; proportional; the number of pages is always 65 times the number of hours.
2. 3, 8, 15, 37.50; proportional; earnings are always 7.5 times the number of hours.
3. Not proportional; the line will not pass through the origin.
4. Proportional; the line will pass through the origin.
5. Yes, the graph will show a proportional relationship because the data for the number of miles traveled and the number of hours will form a straight line and pass through the origin.
6. A: 8 minutes, B: 5 minutes
7. At 0 minutes, or the start of the race, each person has run 0 miles.
8. A: $y = \frac{1}{8}x$, B: $y = \frac{1}{5}x$
9.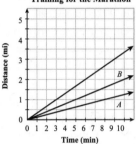

Page 50

1. $0.31
2. $0.44
3. 6¢
4. $1.11
5. 9¢
6. $0.23
7. $1.25
8. $13.40
9. 32¢
10. $0.21; $0.18; 18-oz box
11. $0.60; $0.66; 5-lb bag
12. 30¢; 26¢; 5 paintbrushes for $1.29
13. $1.99; $1.85; pkg of 8 pairs
14. 3 for $3.29
15. 9.4 in.
16. $0.38/lb; $0.61/lb; $0.20/lb; $0.074/oz

Page 51

1. 17, $25\frac{1}{2}$, 34, $42\frac{1}{2}$
2. $\frac{9}{8}$ or $1\frac{1}{8}$
3. $\frac{4}{5}$
4. $\frac{6}{5}$ or $1\frac{1}{5}$
5. 6
6. $2\frac{4}{5}$ miles per hour
7. $\frac{15}{16}$ page per minute
8. $1\frac{1}{2}$ cups per recipe
9. $3\frac{3}{4}$ square yards per hour

Answer Key

Core Skills Math, Grade 7

10. about $2.86 per hour
11. $2.50 per hour
12. Talk Time; their rate per hour is lower
13. Multiply 0.05 times 60 because there are 60 minutes in 1 hour.
14. The unit rate is $3 per hour, so it is not a better deal.

Page 52

1. 5, 10, 15, 20, 30
2. The wall is 30 feet long.
3. 1.5 in.
4. The length is 28 feet and the width is 14 feet. The area is 28 feet × 14 feet, or 392 square feet.
5. The length is 25 meters and the width is 15 meters. The area is 25 meters × 15 meters, or 375 square meters.
6. Check drawings. The rectangle should be 6 units by 4 units.
7. Length is 36 m and width is 24 m using both scales.

Page 53

1–6. Variables chosen will vary.
1. $\frac{1}{6} = \frac{5}{t}$
2. $\frac{1}{6} = \frac{3}{x}$
3. $\frac{1}{6} = \frac{4}{c}$
4. $\frac{1}{6} = \frac{2}{m}$
5. $\frac{1}{6} = \frac{2}{p}$
6. $\frac{1}{6} = \frac{3}{d}$
7–8. Check drawings.
9. Answers will vary.

Page 54

1. 30 ft
2. 18 ft
3. 9 ft
4. 30 ft; 12 ft
5. $6\frac{1}{4}$ yd
6. 3 ft
7. Check problems and drawings.

Page 55

1. 60 cm
2. 135 cm
3. 337.5 cm
4. 5 cm
5. 186 cm
6. 2.6 cm
7. drawing: $3\frac{1}{4}$ in.; actual: 195 ft

8. drawing: $1\frac{3}{4}$ in.; actual: 105 ft
9. 200 ft by 100 ft
10. 64 concrete slabs
11. Check drawing. Rectangle should be 6 cm by 14 cm.

Page 56

1. $x = 14$ cm
2. $x = 4.5$ in.
3. $x = 6$ mm
4. $x = 15$ cm
5. $x = 15$ mm
6. $x = 2$ m
7. $x = 6$ cm
8. $x = 9$ in.
9. yes
10. $2.20/lb
11. about 3
12. about 1
13. about 32
14. about 5

Page 57

1. $x = 4$ cm
2. $x = 3.2$ m
3. $x = 18$ mm
4. $x = 20$ in.
5. $x = 6$ cm
6. $x = 14$ in.
7. $h = 24$ ft
8. 5 dimes, 3 quarters or 10 dimes, 1 quarter
9. 2.5 cm, 4.5 cm, 5.5 cm
10. 10 cm, 18 cm, 22 cm

Page 58

1. 25 feet tall
2. MO is 36 units
3. 32 feet tall
4. QR is 10 units

Page 59

1–4. Check shading.
5. 46%
6. 37%
7. 17%
8. 23%
9. 20%
10. 80%
11. 7%
12. 133%
13. 1%
14. 30%
15. 207%

16. 810%
17. 0.19
18. 0.46
19. 0.02
20. 1.7
21. 0.08
22. 0.89
23. 1.4
24. 0.04
25. 0.31
26. 1.5
27. 0.11
28. 0.03
29. 94%
30. 20 seats
31. more who said they do not watch

Page 60

1. 30%
2. 40%
3. 50%
4. 10%
5. 25%
6. 55%
7. 12%
8. 60%
9. 75%
10. 35%
11. 70%
12. 15%
13. 90%
14. 80%
15. 40%
16. $\frac{3}{10}$
17. $\frac{9}{50}$
18. $\frac{9}{20}$
19. $\frac{7}{25}$
20. $\frac{17}{20}$
21. $\frac{24}{25}$
22. $\frac{39}{100}$
23. $\frac{39}{50}$
24. $\frac{11}{25}$
25. $\frac{13}{20}$
26. $\frac{17}{50}$
27. $\frac{19}{25}$
28. $\frac{22}{25}$
29. $\frac{3}{25}$
30. $\frac{14}{25}$
31. $\frac{6}{25}$
32. $\frac{63}{100}$

144

33. $\frac{11}{100}$

34. $\frac{21}{50}$

35. $\frac{3}{5}$

36. $\frac{27}{50}$

37. $\frac{23}{25}$

38. $\frac{43}{50}$

39. $\frac{7}{50}$

40. $\frac{1}{25}$

41. 75%

42. 8 feet

43. $14.5\% = \frac{145}{1,000} = \frac{29}{200}$; 2.5%
   $= \frac{25}{1,000} = \frac{1}{40}$

Page 61

1. 40%
2. 25%
3. 34%
4. 30%
5. 68%
6. 72%
7. 20%
8. 50%
9. $55\frac{5}{9}\% \approx 55.6\%$
10. 60%
11. 25%
12. 20%
13. $133\frac{1}{3}\%$
14. $15.74
15. $x = 1.9$
16. $z = 12$
17. $c = 2.53$
18. $b = 0.265$

Page 62

1. $2.10
2. $33.15
3. $29.70
4. $19.50
5. $23.55
6. $72.00
7. $0.48
8. $6.75
9. $5.52
10. $3.90
11. $4.82
12. $14.10
13. $68
14. $20.82
15. $250.75
16. $44.84
17. $15.30
18. $425

19. $12.84
20. $9.58
21. $16.59
22. $40.80
23. $30.10
24. Check problems.

Page 63

1–3. Answers will vary.
1. $\frac{40}{100} = \frac{n}{10}$
2. $n\% \times 10 = 7$
3. $0.40 \times n = 4$
4. b
5. a
6. c
7. 90%

Page 64

1. $800 - 600 = 200$; $\frac{200}{800}$; $\frac{1}{4} = 25\%$
2. 80% increase
3. 90% decrease
4. 0.4% decrease
5. 200% increase
6. 1,500 more students

Page 65

1. $33\frac{1}{3}\%$ increase
2. 50% increase
3. 40% decrease
4. 100% increase
5. 62.5% decrease
6. 10% decrease
7. $33\frac{1}{3}\%$ increase
8. 20% decrease
9. 15% increase
10. 2% increase
11. 30% decrease
12. 10% increase
13. 50% increase
14. 20% decrease
15. $1,480.80
16. $8,391.20

Page 66

1. $75
2. $24
3. $33.75
4. $445.20
5. $87.30
6. $75.60
7. $126
8. $18.80
9. $13.30
10. $31.50

11. $48
12. $24.75
13. $I = \$960$; $A = \$4,960$
14. 6 mo
15–19. Estimates may vary.
15. about 900
16. about 100
17. about 50%
18. about 25%
19. about 20%

Page 67

1. 2
2. -4
3. 0
4. -3
5. -1
6. -1
7. 11
8. -20
9. 0
10. -25
11. 54
12. -3
13. 12
14. 10
15. 3
16. -6
17. -10
18. 1
19. 35
20. -10
21. -6
22. 22
23. -9
24. -10°C
25. $\frac{7}{12}$ yd
26. $a = b = 0$ or $a = -b$

Page 68

1. lower than zero
2. negative
3. -2
4. negative
5. -4
6. 7
7. 18
8. -24
9 -19
10. -4
11. 5
12. -4
13. 7
14. -10

145

15. 10
16. 24
17. -4
18. 10
19. 18
20. 0
21. -5
22. 1
23. 12
24. $\frac{33}{4}$ or $8\frac{1}{4}$
25. $\frac{2}{3}$
26. $4\frac{8}{9}$
27. 4
28. 10 in.²
29. 20 m²
30. 2 cm²
31. 12.56 m² or $12\frac{4}{7}$ m²

Page 69

1. 7
2. -7
3. -5
4. 5
5. -7
6. -8
7. 3
8. -9
9. 2
10. -8
11. 11
12. 45
13. 20
14. 0
15. 10
16. -8
17. -23
18. 3
19. 0
20. 16
21. 52
22. 16
23. -39
24. 17
25. 117
26. -14
27. -69
28. -148
29. 15
30. 15
31. -38
32. 0
33. -6
34. 1

35. -7 m
36. 1,552 customers
37. -19, -14, -9, -4, 1, 6
38. 16 in.
39. -10 and -13; -10

Page 70

1. ●●
   ■■■■
   2, 4, 2, 2
2. ●●
   ■■■■
   2, 2
3. 2, 2; 4 + -2 = -2 + 4
4. 4
5. -10
6. 10
7. 6 + (-8) = -2
8. (-8) + 6 = -2
9. 8 + 6 = 14
10. -4

Page 71

1. b
2. by adding 1 gray counter
3. -5
4. -1
5. -10
6. 5
7. 5
8. -1
9. -4
10. -6 + 12; 6
11. -8 + -6; -14
12. 12 + -5; 7
13. 19 + -9; 10
14. -6 + -10; -16
15. 7 + 5; 12
16. Check problems.

Page 72

1. 4
2. 6
3. -5
4. 15
5. 19
6. 14
7. -7
8. 24
9. 6
10. 4
11. -4
12. -6
13. 5

14. -5
15. -1
16. -6
17. -8
18. 2
19. -13
20. 0
21. 0
22. 19°C
23. $3.49
24. -101
25. 119
26. -582
27. 65

Page 73

1. 17
2. 8
3. -6
4. -6
5. 22
6. -42
7. 8
8. 5
9. 16
10. -11
11. 63
12. -14
13. 8
14. 102
15. -22
16. 0
17. 31
18. -118
19. -28
20. 16
21. 3
22. -28
23. 122
24. 0
25. -9
26. -17
27. 0
28. 30 ft higher
29. 118 m
30. -4, -5
31. $\frac{2}{15}$
32. >
33. <
34. >
35. >
36. <
37. <
38. >
39. >

Page 74

1. 4
2. -2
3. -9
4. -26
5. 6
6. 26
7. -10
8. 20
9. -6
10. -16
11. 22
12. -6
13. -19
14. 35
15. -29
16. 25
17. -4
18. -10
19. -11
20. 7
21. -15
22. -1
23. -5
24. 28
25. 2
26. -9
27. -23
28. -14
29. -12
30. -12
31. 4 yd
32. -24°C
33. 3 points
34. 6°C
35. Check Problems

Page 75

1. -3 + (-3) + (-3) = -9

2. -10, -15, -20, -25
3. -27, -18, -9, 0
4. 6, 9, 12, 15, 18
5. 24
6. -24
7. -24
8. 28
9. -28
10. -28
11. -27
12. -3
13. 1
14. -4, 16
15. -5, -5, -5, -125
16. -52, -48, -44
17. Add 4 to each term, or notice that -64 = -16 × 4, -60 = -15 × 4, -56 = -14 × 4 and so on.

Page 76

1. 32
2. -32
3. -78
4. -126
5. -21
6. -34
7. -120
8. -90
9. 54
10. -90
11. 153
12. -54
13. 66
14. -39
15. 50
16. -126
17. -68
18. 120
19. -81
20. -36
21. 24
22. 144
23. -80
24. -220
25. -90
26. 150
27. -120
28. 8
29. 40
30. 78
31. -36
32. 72
33. -198
34. $25
35. -8 and 7
36. 410 cans

Page 77

1. 7
2. -6
3. -9
4. -9
5. 9
6. -11
7. 9
8. 0
9. -5
10. -7
11. 4
12. 1
13. -4
14. 8
15. 9
16. 2
17. -5
18. 36
19. -5
20. -2
21. 4
22. -2.5°C
23. $56.25
24. 20 pounds
25. 20%
26. 82°; 172°
27. 54°; 144°
28. 1°; 91°
29. 49°; 139°
30. 25°; 115°
31. 17°; 107°

Page 78

1. -11
2. -3
3. -5
4. 33
5. -12
6. 22
7. -25
8. -30
9. -7
10. 12
11. -14
12. -8
13. -66
14. 4
15. 79
16. -156
17. 100
18. -24
19. 50 days

20. 24 in. shorter
21. *n*
22. *n*
23. $200

Page 79

1. Distributive Property of Multiplication over Addition
2. Commutative and Associative Properties of Addition
3. Associative Property of Multiplication
4. -6
5. -16
6. 0
7. 1
8. -1
9. 8
10. -13
11 -23
12. 2
13. -6
14. $-3 \cdot 4; -3 \cdot -5; -12 + 15 = 3$
15. 12 years old
16. $22
17. 3 and -8

Page 80

1. 0.15
2. 0.98
3. 2.25
4. 0.65
5. 2.6
6. 0.042
7. 0.62
8. 0.25
9. 0.32
10. 0.75
11. 3.6
12. 0.89
13. 0.635
14. 0.22
15. 0.35
16. 2.3
17. piano
18. $\frac{3}{8}$
19. 63/100
20. 10.375 cm long and 8.25 cm wide
21. 6.25%
22. 31.25%
23. 43.75%

Page 81

1. $0.1111111\ldots, 0.\overline{1}$
2. $0.\overline{2}$
3. $0.\overline{5}$
4. $1.\overline{1}$
5. $0.0\overline{2}$
6. $0.\overline{263}$
7. $0.381\overline{244}$
8. $3.\overline{113}$
9. $3.129\overline{831}$
10. $0.41\overline{6}$
11. $1.\overline{6}$
12. $2.\overline{6}$
13. $2.\overline{4}$
14. $1.\overline{1}$
15. $0.58\overline{3}$
16. $0.\overline{36}$
17. $0.3\overline{8}$
18. $3.\overline{3}$
19. $1.\overline{2}$
20. $0.0\overline{1}$
21. $\frac{2}{27} = 0.\overline{074}; \frac{4}{27} = 0.\overline{148}; \frac{8}{27} = 0.\overline{296};$ $\frac{10}{27} = 0.\overline{370}; \frac{20}{27} = 0.\overline{740};$ $\frac{80}{27} = 2.\overline{962}$

Page 82

1. terminating; 0.2125
2. terminating; 0.78125
3. repeating; $0.3958\overline{3}$
4. $-0.91\overline{6}$
5. -5
6. $3.\overline{6}$
7. 5.125
8. 0.22
9. $0.\overline{7}$
10. terminating; 0.3125
11. terminating; 0.036
12. terminating; 0.12
13. repeating; $0.\overline{54}$
14. repeating: $0.2\overline{7}$
15. repeating; $0.4\overline{6}$
16. repeating: $1.\overline{2}$
17. repeating; $0.\overline{18}$
18. terminating; 0.6
19. $-\frac{3}{4}; -0.75$
20. $-\frac{1}{10}; -0.1$
21. $\frac{1}{4}, 0.25$
22. $\frac{19}{20}; 0.95$

Page 83

1. $\frac{3}{4}$, left, negative, 0, the overall change is 0 cups
2. -5
3. -4
4. $4 + (-6) = -2$
5. $-3 + 4 = 1$
6. -15
7. -27.4
8. -30
9. -18
10. 2
11. -25
12. Answers will vary. Possible answer: A football team lost 10 yards on a play. On the next play they lost another 2 yards. -12; the total number of yards lost in 2 plays.

Page 84

1. 13
2. -8
3. -11
4. -4
5. -36
6. -7.7
7. 1
8. 79
9. $2\frac{7}{9}$
10. $78\frac{1}{2}$
11. $-1 - 0.5 = -1.5$; 1.5 meters below sea level
12. $-12 - 5 = -17$; total loss 17 yards
13. $533 - (-10) = 543$; 543 feet
14. $-15 - 12 = -27$; -27°C
15. $-20 - (-12) = -8$; 8°C
16. $-45.00 - 30.15 = -75.15$; $75.15
17. $|-61.5 - (-23.4)| = |-38.1| = 38.1$; 38.1 units

Page 85

1. -9
2. $\frac{24}{35}$
3. 54
4. -100
5. -60
6. -157.2
7. $-2\frac{4}{5}$
8. 0
9. -96
10. $7(-75) = -525$; $525
11. $3(-5) = -15$; 15 yards

148

12. $6(-2) = -12$; 12°F
13. $(-\frac{1}{4})(5) = -1\frac{1}{4}$; $1\frac{1}{4}$ miles
14. $4(-3.50) = -14$; $14
15. $18(-100) = -1,800$; $1,800
16. Answers will vary. Possible answer: A stock dropped 34 points each day for 3 days. How many points did the stock drop over the 3 days? $-34(3) = -102$; the stock dropped 102 points.

Page 86

1. -0.8
2. $-\frac{1}{7}$
3. -8
4. $-\frac{502}{3}$ or $-167\frac{1}{3}$
5. -375
6. 7
7. $-\frac{4}{21}$
8. -400
9. -1.3
10. -20
11. $-\frac{32}{9}$ or $-3\frac{5}{9}$
12. 20
13. $-45 \div 5 = -9$; $9 per day, on average
14. $-225 \div 5 = -45$; 45 yards
15. Yes, it is a rational number because $1\frac{1}{4}$ can be written as $\frac{5}{4}$, which is a ratio of two integers, and the denominator is not zero.
16. Yes, since an integer divided by an integer is a ratio of two integers and the denominator is not zero, the number is rational by definition.
17. Answers will vary. Possible Answer: The temperature dropped 85° over 15 days. Find the average change in temperature per day. $-85 \div 15 = -5.67$; the average change in temperature was -5.67 degrees per day.

Page 87

1–2. Check diagrams.
1. 8 possibilities
2. 6 possibilities
3. 3 quarts
4. They picked the same amount.
5. $\frac{1}{6}$
6. $\frac{1}{6}$
7. $\frac{1}{4}$

8. $\frac{5}{12}$
9. $\frac{1}{2}$
10. $\frac{5}{6}$
11. $\frac{13}{4}$ or $3\frac{1}{4}$
12. $\frac{2}{9}$
13. $\frac{53}{7}$ or $7\frac{4}{7}$
14. $2\frac{2}{3}$
15. $2\frac{3}{4}$

Page 88

1–3. Check diagrams
4. 6 choices
5. 12 choices
6. 32 choices
7. 35 choices
8. 35 watches
9. 20 shows
10. 16 sentences

Page 89

1. (H, T), (H, R), (H, S), (H, L), (H, P)
2. (T, H), (T, R), (T, S), (T, L), (T, P); (R, H), (R, T), (R, S), (R, L), (R, P); (S, H), (S, T), (S, R), (S, L), (S, P); (L, H), (L, T), (L, R), (L, S), (L, P); (P, H), (P, T), (P, R), (P, S), (P, L)
3. 15 pairs
4. $5 + 4 + 3 + 2 + 1 = 15$
5. 28 combinations
6. 10 triangles

Page 90

1. 5 choices
2. 4 seats
3. 3 seats
4. 2 seats
5. 1 seat
6. 120 arrangements; yes; For each seat filled, the number of ways of filling the next seat is one less.
7. 5,040 ways
8. 720 orders
9. 6,720 results
10. 120
11. 720
12. 5,040
13. 362,880

Page 91

1. $\frac{1}{5}$
2. $\frac{4}{5}$
3. $\frac{9}{25}$
4. $\frac{4}{25}$
5. $12
6. 56 ways
7. Answers may vary.

Page 92

1. 6
2. 2
3. 4
4. 9
5. 18
6. 6
7. 3
8. 300
9. $1.20
10. Check answers.

Page 93

1. yes
2. no
3. no
4. no
5. neither
6. certain
7. 3:4 or $\frac{3}{4}$
8. 38.5%
9. 1:2 or $\frac{1}{2}$
10. 1 and 6, 2 and 5, 3 and 4

Page 94

1. $\frac{1}{8}$
2. $\frac{1}{8}$
3. $\frac{1}{2}$
4. $\frac{1}{4}$
5. $\frac{3}{4}$
6. $\frac{7}{8}$
7. $\frac{1}{2}$
8. $\frac{3}{8}$
9. $\frac{1}{8}$
10. $\frac{2}{5}$
11. $\frac{1}{5}$
12. Answers will vary.

Answer Key
Core Skills Math, Grade 7

Page 95

1. $\frac{3}{10}$
2. red, blue, or green
3. $\frac{2}{5}$
4. yes; It is only $\frac{1}{10}$ less than $\frac{2}{5}$.
5. yes; 22 out of 50 is close to 20 out of 50.
6. 200 times
7. 5 times
8. 25 times
9. 12 times
10. 20 times
11. 36 hits

Page 96

1. 12; 5
2. red, green, blue, yellow, and white
3. $\frac{2}{12}; \frac{4}{12}; \frac{1}{12}$
4. $\frac{8}{12}$
5. Jack, Jim, Juan, Joe, and Joel
6. $\frac{3}{8}; \frac{5}{8}; 0$
7. 1 time
8. 3 times
9. 1 time
10. 2 times
11. Check answers.

Page 97

1. white, blue, red, yellow
2. red
3. $\frac{5}{80}$ or $\frac{1}{16}$
4. $\frac{40}{80}$ or $\frac{1}{2}$
5. $\frac{25}{80}$ or $\frac{5}{16}$
6. $\frac{10}{80}$ or $\frac{1}{8}$
7. $\frac{30}{80}$ or $\frac{3}{8}$
8. $\frac{80}{80}$ or $\frac{1}{1}$
9. $\frac{2}{7}$
10. 5:2
11. 48 ft, 144 ft²
12. 29 in., 51 in.²
13. 113 cm, 450 cm²

Page 98

1. 16, 20; 3, 4; $\frac{3}{16}, \frac{4}{20} = \frac{1}{5}$
2. Basket B has the better chance of winning.
3. $\frac{1}{2}$; 0.50; 50%
4. $\frac{4}{9}$
5. $\frac{5}{9}$

6. You could find the complement of Exercise 4; $1 - \frac{4}{9} = \frac{5}{9}$; or you could find the theoretical probability.
   $$\frac{\text{number of girls}}{\text{total number of students}} = \frac{15}{27} = \frac{5}{9}$$
7. 10
8. 94
9. 25
10. The chances of landing on an even number are $\frac{1}{2}$. The chances of landing on an odd number are $\frac{1}{2}$. Therefore, the probability of landing on an odd number is the same as the probability of landing on an even number.

Page 99

1. Check tables.
2. The probability would be close to the theoretical probability of $\frac{1}{2}$.
3. $\frac{6}{35}; \frac{13}{70}; \frac{9}{35}; \frac{17}{70}; \frac{1}{7}$
4. $\frac{1}{6}$
5. Check tables.
6. Answers will vary. Possible answer: The experimental probabilities are fairly close to the theoretical probabilities.
7. $\frac{5}{12}$ or about 41.7% of the time the dog does not want to go out between 4 P.M. and 5 P.M.

Page 100

1.

	1	2	3	4	5	6
1	1	2	3	4	5	6
2	2	4	6	8	10	12
3	3	6	9	12	15	18
4	4	8	12	16	20	24
5	5	10	15	20	25	30
6	6	12	18	24	30	36

2. $\frac{15}{36}$ or $\frac{5}{12}$
3. $\frac{23}{36}$
4.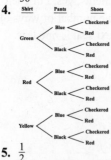
5. $\frac{1}{2}$

6. 222, 223, 228, 232, 233, 238,
   282, 283, 288, 322, 323, 328,
   332, 333, 338, 382, 383, 388,
   822, 823, 828, 832, 833, 838,
   882, 883, 888
7. $\frac{19}{27}$

Page 101

1. Check diagrams.
2. $\frac{1}{9}$ or 1 out of 9
3. cake
4. 16 outfits
5. 10
6. 6.72
7. division; $z = 10$
8. multiplication; $m = 546$
9–10. Pictures will vary. Number of choices is given.
9. 8
10. 9

Page 102

1. $\frac{1}{24}$
2. $\frac{1}{24}$
3. $\frac{5}{24}$
4. $\frac{1}{8}$
5. 0
6. 0
7. $\frac{1}{36}$
8. $\frac{1}{12}$
9. $\frac{1}{12}$
10. $\frac{1}{4}$
11. $\frac{5}{36}$
12. $\frac{1}{72}$
13. $\frac{5}{108}$
14. $\frac{1}{9}$
15. $\frac{3}{4} \times 96 = 72$
16. $\frac{21}{50} \times 100 = 42$
17. $\frac{9}{100} \times 40 = 3.6$
18. $0.05 \times 36 = 1.8$
19. $0.12 \times 500 = 60$
20. $0.035 \times 500 = 17.5$

Page 103

1. $\frac{1}{24}$
2. $\frac{1}{4}$
3. $\frac{1}{8}$
4. $\frac{5}{24}$
5. 0
6. $\frac{1}{6}$

7. $\frac{1}{32}$
8. $\frac{1}{16}$
9. $\frac{3}{8}$
10. $\frac{7}{16}$
11. $\frac{1}{32}$
12. $\frac{1}{16}$
13. $\frac{1}{2}$
14. 35 questions
15. $\frac{1}{8}$
16. $\frac{2}{15}$
17. $\frac{17}{6}$ or $2\frac{5}{6}$
18. mean: 80; median: 79; mode: 73

Page 104

1. $\frac{1}{11}$
2. $\frac{3}{44}$
3. $\frac{2}{33}$
4. $\frac{1}{11}$
5. $\frac{1}{22}$
6. $\frac{1}{22}$
7. $\frac{1}{66}$
8. $\frac{1}{11}$
9. 0
10. $\frac{3}{44}$
11. $\frac{2}{21}$
12. $\frac{2}{21}$
13. $\frac{8}{105}$
14. $\frac{5}{17}$
15. 15 ways: $\frac{1}{1}, \frac{1}{2}, \frac{1}{4}, \frac{1}{6}, \frac{1}{8}, \frac{2}{1}, \frac{2}{6}, \frac{4}{1}, \frac{4}{6}, \frac{6}{1},$
    $\frac{6}{2}, \frac{6}{4}, \frac{8}{1}, \frac{8}{6}, \frac{6}{8}$

Page 105

1. $\frac{1}{15}$
2. $\frac{1}{9}$
3. $\frac{2}{9}$
4. $\frac{1}{12}$
5. $\frac{1}{60}$
6. $\frac{1}{120}$
7. $\frac{1}{24}$
8. $\frac{1}{14}$
9. $\frac{1}{6}$
10. $\frac{1}{26}$
11. $\frac{1}{13}$
12. $\frac{1}{13}$
13. $\frac{1}{17}$
14. Check question.

Page 106

1. 13 names
2. Check problems.
3. 100 combinations
4. 12 bananas
5. 300 passengers
6. 3 children
7. Check problems.

Page 107

1–2. Answers will vary.
3. total number of birds at large in the population
4. Assign each spinner item a digit. The probability of any item occurring is the number of times its digit occurs in the sample of random numbers, divided by 20. This ratio, multiplied by 100, will simulate the number of times the spinner item would be selected randomly in 100 spins.
5. 40%
6. 24
7. 6
8. 50
9. 1,200
10. 42

Page 108

1. The run can be used as a simulation to determine what percentage of stamping errors occurred during the 3-hour run.
2. about 900 cans
3. about 3,000 cans
4. about 600 cans
5. 256 ways
6. about 2,400 cans
7. $\frac{3}{512}$ or 0.00586

Page 109

1. $\frac{7}{10}$
2. $\frac{1}{2}$
3. $\frac{2}{5}$
4. $\frac{2}{5}$

Page 110

1. U
2. $\overline{VY}, \overline{XZ}$
3. Possible answers: $\overline{VU}, \overline{WU}$
4. Possible answers: $\overline{ZY}, \overline{VY}$
5. $\odot U$
6. Possible answers: $\overline{XZ}, \overline{XY}$
7. 10 cm; 5 cm
8. diameter of the large circle
9. diameter of the small circle
10. radius of the large circle
11. radius of the small circle
12. 50 ft
13. 24 bricks
14. 0.45
15. 0.36
16. 0.05
17. 0.4
18. $\frac{2}{5}$
19. $\frac{3}{4}$
20. $\frac{13}{20}$
21. $\frac{9}{25}$

Page 111

1. 44 in.
2. 132 in.
3. 88 in.
4. 88 in.
5. 44 cm
6. 132 ft
7. 18.8 m
8. 75.4 cm
9. 56.5 in.
10. 6.3 m
11. 22.0 ft
12. 56.5 mm
13. 12.6 cm
14. 28.3 in.
15. 94.2 m
16. 56.5 cm
17. 113.0 ft
18. 125.6 mm
19. Answers will vary, but should mention using the memory key.

Page 112

1. 6.28 cm
2. 43.96 in.
3. 37.68 m
4. 94.2 ft
5. 28 m
6. 7 cm
7. 38 cm
8. 46 mm
9. 176 m
10. 198 m
11. 18 cm
12. 26 cm
13. 20.1 mm
14. 5.0 cm
15. 35.2 cm
16. 66.3 m
17. 4 m
18. 9 ft
19. -9

Page 113

1. 25.47 cm
2. 0.19 cm
3. 1.51 m
4. 2.89 km
5. 44 in.
6. 132 yd
7. 176 ft
8. 220 ft
9. 42 ft
10. 0.5 m
11. 100 in.
12. perimeter of the square
13. 9.42 m
14. 31.4 ft
15. 20 cm
16. 80 m
17. 16 km
18. 24 cm
19. 28 yd
20. 21
21. -54
22. 56

Page 114

1. 2.1 m
2. 22 in.
3. 241.78 mm
4. 769.3 cm
5. $180
6. $180
7. 22.2 mph

8. 7 mm
9. 20 flowers

Page 115

1. 314 in.^{2}
2. 50.2 in.^{2}
3. 78.5 m^2
4. 28.3 ft^2
5. 7.1 in.^{2}
6. 32.2 cm^2
7. 2.5 m^2
8. 651.1 in.^{2}
9. 38.5 cm^2
10. 63.6 ft^2
11. 176.6 m^2
12. 1,589.6 in.^{2}
13. about 144.4 cm
14. about 31,400 mi^2
15. about 18 in.
16. 1,884 ft^2
17. about 6,594 ft^2

Page 116

1. 314 cm^2
2. 5 cm^2
3. 64 m^2
4. 333 cm^2
5. 7 m^2
6. 53 cm^2
7. 660 m^2
8. 475 m^2
9. 12.6 m^2
10. 254.3 m^2
11. 113.0 m^2
12. 2.01 in.^{2}
13. 1.54 ft^2
14. 0.41 m^2
15. 78.5 in.^{2}
16. 392.5 in^2
17. 5
18. 5, 7, 3, 4

Page 117

1. 50.24 cm^2
2. 314 m^2
3. 191.04 m^2
4. 241.78 cm^2
5. 150.72 cm^2
6. 34.24 in.^{2}
7. 78.5 m^2
8. 37.68 in.
9. 80
10. 22
11. 5

12. 21
13. 1.5
14. 0.16
15. 0.06
16. 0.5

Page 118

1–2. Check student's work.
3. Answers will vary. Possible answer: $\frac{C}{d}$ is always close to or a little more than 3.
4. C, 2π; C, 2π; C, 2, π; π, C, 4, π; C, 4, π; π, A; $4\pi A$
5. 16π square units
6. $\frac{\pi}{4}$ square units
7. π square units

Page 119

1. 108 cm^2
2. 49 in.^{2}
3. 252 cm^2
4. 63 cm^2
5. 96 m^2
6. 147 in.^{2}
7. 90 cm^2
8. 56 cm^2
9. 54 cm^2
10. 99 in.^{2}
11. 5 ft^2
12. 17 peonies
13. 9 cans
14. 94 in.^{2}

Page 120

1. 34 m^2
2. 144 cm^2
3. 40 cm^2
4. 150 m^2
5. 176 m^2
6. 105 m^2
7. 50 cm^2
8. 70 m^2
9. 1,200 cm^2
10. 94.5 in.^{2}
11. 39 in.^{2}
12. 14 cm
13.
14.

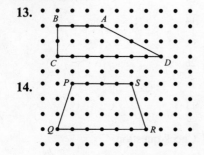

Answer Key
Core Skills Math, Grade 7

Page 121

1. 2 right triangles, 1 rectangle
2. 6 m²; 6 m²; 48 m²
3. 60 m²
4. 2 rectangles
5. by subtracting area of small rectangle from area of large rectangle
6. 104 ft²
7. 174 in.²
8. 34.5 m²
9. 20 ft²
10. Possible answer: Use addition when the irregular figure is made up of simpler figures; use subtraction when the irregular figure is only part of a larger simpler figure.

Page 122

1. 34 square units
2. 72 cm²
3. about 84.56 m²
4. 288 sq cm; check work.
5. $97.88
6. 5 ft

Page 123

1. sphere
2. cylinder
3. cone
4. sphere
5. cone
6. cylindrical; easy to hold
7. spherical; can roll
8. 7.85 inches
9. 3.34 inches
10. 4.00×10^7 m
11. 2.40×10^9 m
12. 9.42×10^{11} m

Page 124

1.
2.
3.
4.

5. 40 cubes; 27 cubes
6.
7. Check drawings.

Page 125

1. triangle
2. rectangle
3. parallelogram
4. rectangle
5. rectangle; triangle
6. rectangle, triangle, trapezoid
7. rectangle, circle, oval
8. 1; circle

Page 126

1. 54 units²
2. 48 units²
3. 160 in.²
4. 1,032 cm²
5. 7, 12, 18, 12, 18, 7, 150
6. 434 m²
7. 54.5 yd²

Page 127

1. 108 cm²
2. 704 m²
3. 360 mm²
4. 228 cm²
5. 486 m²
6. 195 cm²
7. 54 in.²
8. 465 ft²
9. 8 cubes, 12 cubes, 6 cubes, 1 cube

Page 128

1. 42 cm³
2. 24 cm³
3. 360 ft³
4. 385 cm³
5. 40,000 ft³
6. The triangular prism container is the better deal because the volume is 192 cubic inches and the rectangular prism holds only 180 cubic inches.

7. Yes, different rectangular prisms can have different heights and the same volume. Possible answers:

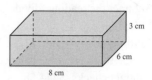

$V = (8)(6)(3) = 144$ cm³

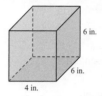

$V = (4)(6)(6) = 144$ cm³

Page 129

1. 1,800 in.³
2. 3 m³
3. 6.6m³
4. 10 m³
5. 880 cm³
6. 6 ft³
7. 4.5 cm³
8. 9 m³
9. 22.8 m³
10. 10 cm × 10 cm × 10 cm
11. 104.58 m³
12. Multiply 6 times the length squared.

Page 130

1. about $130; $131.39
2. about 4; $4.28
3. about 4 min; 4.26 min
4. about 200 km; 177 km
5. about $1,050; $1,037.25
6. about 5,500 miles; 5,479 miles
7. $3.98
8. $399.45
9. $498.97
10. $1,130.10

Answer Key
Core Skills Math, Grade 7

Page 131

1. Find amount remaining; divide by $3; 56 subscriptions
2. Subtract the reading; divide by 2. 113.65 mi
3. Multiply $5 by 4; add $12. $32
4. Add $100 to previous balance; subtract checks. $274.58
5. $21.89
6. $511.15
7. Check problems.

Page 132

1. 728 passengers
2. $82.75
3. $32.45 each
4. $10,299.82
5. $96.25 in all
6. 29 bags
7. $380 for 5 nights
8. 5 cans
9. 3, 7, 5
10. 1, 2, 5, 8, 9

Page 133

1. $80
2. $154.40
3. $95.60; $79.40
4. Answers and reasons will vary. Possible answer: Rent because it is the least expensive option.
5. about $800
6. $49

Page 134

1. $6\frac{3}{4}$ hr
2. 12 games
3. 2 mi
4. 26 fence posts
5. First row: $\frac{5}{2}$; second row: $\frac{1}{4}, \frac{1}{2}$; third row: $\frac{1}{20}, \frac{1}{10}$; last row: $\frac{1}{50}, \frac{1}{25}$
6. Answers will vary. Possible answers: Start with $\frac{5}{4}$, multiply by $\frac{2}{5}$; start with $\frac{1}{100}$, multiply by 10.

Page 135

1. $9\frac{7}{8}$ ft; $12\frac{5}{8}$
2. 4 sections
3. 2 blocks
4. 44 cows
5. $5\frac{1}{4}$ ft
6. 8 dimes and 3 nickels
7. about 11 hr
8. $93

Page 136

1. 764 students
2. $18.75 per hour
3. 1,296 people
4. The digit is 9.
5. 5.4×10^{-1}
6. 243 employees

154

Answer Key
Core Skills Math, Grade 7